# Advice to Young Men and Boys

STEPHEN GIRARD.

# Advice
# to
# Young men and Boys

## A Series of Addresses

Delivered by

# B. B. Comegys

## Illustrated

**Ross & Perry, Inc.**
Washington, D.C.

© Ross & Perry, Inc. 2002 on new material. All rights reserved.

Protected under the Berne Convention.

Printed in The United States of America

Ross & Perry, Inc. Publishers
216 G St., N.E.
Washington, D.C. 20002
Telephone (202) 675-8300
Facsimile (801) 459-7535
info@RossPerry.com

SAN 253-8555

Library of Congress Control Number: 2002105377
http://www.rossperry.com

ISBN 1-932080-18-X

Book Cover designed by Sapna. sapna@rossperry.com

☉ The paper used in this publication meets the requirements for permanence
established by the American National Standard for Information Sciences
"Permanence of Paper for Printed Library Materials" (ANSI Z39.48-1984).

All rights reserved. No copyrighted part of this publication may be reproduced,
stored in a retrieval system, or transmitted, in any form or by any means,
electronic, photocopying, recording, or otherwise, without the prior written
permission of the publisher.

# PREFACE TO THE EDITION OF 1908.

THIS volume of Addresses by the late Mr. B. B. Comegys is now published by the Board of Directors of City Trusts, and a copy is given to every Girard College boy when he leaves the Institution.

Mr. Comegys served Girard College in two capacities. As a Director of the Board of City Trusts he was a member of the Board of Management. As a Sunday Chapel speaker he was one of the moral and religious instructors. He was appointed to the former position January 7, 1882. He made his first address at the chapel service February 23, 1873.

It was his interest in boys and young men that first drew him to Girard College. From his own early life and experience he knew what life meant for them; what was in store for them for good and for evil; its opportunities and its temptations. He knew their trials, and so had for them a true and abiding sympathy.

It is characteristic of Mr. Comegys that in his Addresses he asked young men to do nothing but what he himself had done or was doing. Did he ask them to read good books? He read them himself, and no others. Did he ask them to practice industry, punctuality, and to do with their might whatever fell to their lot to do? He was only asking them to do what he had done in his earlier years. He says of himself: "When I was twenty-one years of age I had a situation in a store where there was no porter, and I did all the work. I swept the store; I swept the pavement to the curbstone; I made the fires." Did he urge them to be moderate in all things, and abstemious, and to avoid the pleasures of sense that weaken the body and contaminate the mind? His advice was supplemented by his own life. He had attained to fourscore years in the full possession of all his faculties, not so much by reason of strength as by reason of virtue and of moderation. His life was a life of industry and integrity, application and education. He demonstrated in himself the truth that man's education is the work of a lifetime, beginning with consciousness and ending only with the loss of the faculties.

The Board of Directors of City Trusts therefore feel that in continuing the publication of these Addresses they are conferring a lasting benefit on the many young men who will read them and be benefited by them, and at the same time be paying a tribute to the worth of their late highly respected colleague.

# PREFACE.

IN January, 1882, I was appointed by the Judges of the Courts of Common Pleas of Philadelphia to the Board of Directors of City Trusts, which has charge of Girard College, having for some years previously, by the kind partiality of President Allen, been on the staff of speakers in the Chapel on Sundays. My interest in the Pupils was of course at once increased, and ever since I have given much time and thought to the moral instruction of the boys.

From the many Addresses made to them I have selected the following as fair specimens of the instruction I have sought to impart. Some repetitions of thought and language may be accounted for by the lapse of time between the giving of the Addresses, not forgetting the well-known Hebrew proverb, "Line upon line—precept upon precept—here a little—there a little."

The word "Orphans" as used in the will of Mr. Girard has been defined by the Supreme Court of Pennsylvania to mean boys who are fatherless.

The book is published in the hope that it may be the means of helping some boys and young men other than those to whom the Addresses were made.

>4205 WALNUT ST.,
>*November*, 1889.

# CONTENTS.

| | |
|---|---|
| STEPHEN GIRARD AND HIS COLLEGE. (Introductory) . PAGE | 9 |
| HOW TO WIN SUCCESS . . . . . . . " | 25 |
| LIFE—ITS OPPORTUNITIES AND TEMPTATIONS . . . " | 39 |
| ON THE DEATH OF WILLIAM WELSH . . . . " | 51 |
| BAD ASSOCIATES . . . . . . . . " | 59 |
| ON THE DEATH OF PRESIDENT GARFIELD . . . " | 69 |
| THE CASE OF THE UNEDUCATED EMPLOYED . . . " | 79 |
| WILLIAM PENN . . . . . . . . " | 99 |
| OUR CONSTITUTION . . . . . . . " | 113 |
| JAMES LAWRENCE CLAGHORN . . . . . . " | 129 |
| THE LEAF TURNED OVER . . . . . . " | 143 |
| THANKSGIVING DAY. (November 29, 1888) . . . " | 155 |
| ON THE DEATH OF PRESIDENT ALLEN . . . . " | 169 |
| A YOUNG MAN'S MESSAGE TO BOYS . . . . " | 179 |
| A TRUTHFUL CHARACTER . . . . . . " | 188 |

## LIST OF PHOTOGRAVURE ILLUSTRATIONS.

STEPHEN GIRARD . . . . . . *Frontispiece.*

B. B. COMEGYS . . . . . . . PAGE 25

WILLIAM HENRY ALLEN . . . . . " 169

# STEPHEN GIRARD AND HIS COLLEGE.*

### INTRODUCTORY.

STEPHEN GIRARD, who calls himself in his will "mariner and merchant," was born near the city of Bordeaux, France, on May 20, 1750. At the age of twenty-six he settled in Philadelphia, having his counting house on Water street, above Market. He was a man of great industry and frugality, and lived comfortably, as the merchants of that day lived, in the dwelling of which his counting-house formed a part. He was married and had one child, but the death of his wife was followed soon by the death of his child, and he never married again. He lived to the age of eighty-one and accumulated what was considered at the time of his death a vast estate, more than seven millions of dollars. One hundred and forty thousand dollars of this was bequeathed to members of his family, sixty-five thousand as a principal sum for the payment of annuities to certain friends and former employés, one hundred and sixteen thousand to various Philadelphia chari-

---

* This introduction is taken by permission from "The Life and Character of Stephen Girard, by Henry Atlee Ingram, LL. B."

ties, five hundred thousand to the city of Philadelphia for the improvement of its water front on the Delaware, three hundred thousand to the State of Pennsylvania for the prosecution of internal improvements, and an indefinite sum in various legacies to his apprentices, to sea-captains who should bring his vessels in their charge safely to port, and to his house servants. The remainder of his estate he devised in trust to the city of Philadelphia for the following purposes: (1) To erect, improve and maintain a college for poor white orphan boys; (2) to establish a better police system, and (3) to improve the city of Philadelphia and diminish taxation.

The sum of two millions of dollars was set apart by his will for the construction of the college, and as soon as was practicable the executors appropriated certain securities for the purpose, the actual outlay for erection and finishing of the edifice being one million nine hundred and thirty-three thousand eight hundred and twenty-one dollars and seventy-eight cents ($1,933,821.78). Excavation was commenced May 6, 1833, the corner-stone being laid with ceremonies on the Fourth of July following, and the completed buildings were transferred to the Board of Directors on the 13th of November, 1847. There was thus occupied in construction a period of fourteen years and six months, the work being somewhat delayed by reason of suits brought by the heirs of Girard against the city of Philadelphia to recover the estate. The design adopted was substantially that furnished by Thomas U. Walters, an architect elected by the Board of Directors. Some modifications were rendered advisable by the change of site directed in the second codicil of Girard's will, the original purpose having been to occupy the square bounded by Eleventh, Chestnut, Twelfth and Market streets, in the heart of the city of Philadelphia. But Girard having, subsequently to the first draft of his will, purchased for thirty-five thousand dollars the William Parker farm of forty-five acres, on the Ridge Road, known as the "Peel Hall Estate," he directed that the site of his college should be transferred to that place, and commenced the erection of stores and dwellings upon the former plot of ground, which dwellings and stores form part of his residuary estate.

The college proper closely resembles in design a Greek temple. It is built of marble, which was chiefly obtained from quarries in Montgomery and Chester counties, Pennsylvania, and at Egremont, Massachusetts.

The building is three stories in height, the first and second being twenty-five feet from floor to floor, and the third thirty feet in the clear to the eye of the dome, the doors of entrance being in the north and south fronts and measuring sixteen feet in width and thirty-two in height. The walls of the cella are four feet in thickness, and are pierced on each flank by twenty windows. At each end of the building is a vestibule, extending across the whole width of the cella, the ceilings of which are supported on each floor by eight columns, whose shafts are composed of a single stone. Those on the first floor are Ionic, after the temple on the Ilissus, at Athens; on the second, a modified Corinthian, after the Tower of Andronicus Cyrrhestes, also at Athens; and on the third, a similar modification of the Corinthian, somewhat lighter and more ornate.

The auxiliary buildings include a chapel of white marble, dormitories, offices and laundries. A new refectory, containing improved ranges and steam cooking apparatus, has recently been added, the dining-hall of which will seat with ease more than one thousand persons. Two bathing-pools are in the western portion of the grounds, and others in basements of buildings. The houses are heated by steam and lighted by gas obtained from the city works. Thirty-five electric lights from seven towers one hundred and twenty-five feet high illuminate the grounds and the neighboring streets. A wall sixteen inches in thickness and ten feet in height, strengthened by spur piers on the inside and capped with marble coping, surrounds the whole estate, its length being six thousand eight hundred and forty-three feet, or somewhat more than one and one-quarter miles. It is pierced on the southern side, immediately facing the south front of the main building, for the chief entrance.

this last being flanked by two octagonal white marble lodges, between which stretches an ornamental wrought-iron grille, with wrought-iron gates, the whole forming an approach in keeping with the large simplicity of the college itself.

The site upon which the college is erected corresponds well with its splendor and importance. It is elevated considerably above the general level of the surrounding buildings and forms a conspicuous object, not only from the higher windows and roofs in every part of Philadelphia, but from the Delaware river many miles below the city and from eminences far out in the country. From the lofty marble roof the view is also exceedingly beautiful, embracing the city and its environs for many miles around and the course, to their confluence, eight miles below, of the Delaware and Schuylkill rivers.

The history of the institution commences shortly after the decease of Girard, when the Councils of Philadelphia, acting as his trustees, elected a Board of Directors, which organized on the 18th of February, 1833, with Nicholas Biddle as chairman. A Building Committee was also appointed by the City Councils on the 21st of the following March, in whom was vested the immediate supervision of the construction of the college, an office in which they continued without intermission until the final completion of the structure.

On the 19th of July, 1836, the former body, having previously been authorized by the Councils so to do, proceeded to elect Alexander Dallas Bache president of the college, and instructed him to visit various similar institutions in Europe, and purchase the necessary books and apparatus for the school, both of which he did, making an exhaustive report upon his return in 1838. It was then attempted to establish schools without awaiting the completion of the main building, but competent legal advice being unfavorable to the organization of the institution prior to that time, the idea was abandoned, and difficulties having meanwhile arisen between the Councils and the Board of Directors, the ordinances creating the board and authorizing the election of the president were repealed.

In June, 1847, a new board was appointed, to whom the building was transferred, and on December 15, 1847, the officers of the institution were elected, the Hon. Joel Jones, President Judge of the District Court for the City and County of Philadelphia, being chosen as president. On January 1, 1848, the college was opened with a class of one hundred orphans, previously admitted, the occasion being signalized by appropriate ceremonies. On October 1 of the same year one hundred more were admitted, and on April 1, 1849, an additional one hundred, since when others have been admitted as vacancies have occurred or to swell the number as facilities have increased. The college now (1889) contains thirteen hundred and seventy-five pupils.

On June 1, 1849, Judge Jones resigned the office of president of the college, and on the 23d of the following November William H. Allen, LL. D., Professor of Mental Philosophy and English Literature in Dickinson College, was elected to fill the vacancy. He was installed January 1, 1850, but resigned December 1, 1862, and Major Richard Somers Smith, of the United States army, was chosen to fill his place. Major Smith was inaugurated June 24, 1863, and resigned in September, 1867, Dr. Allen being immediately re-elected and continuing in office until his death, on the 29th of August, 1882.

The present incumbent, Adam H. Fetterolf, Ph. D., LL. D., was elected December 27, 1882, by the Board of City Trusts. This Board is composed of fifteen members, three of whom—the Mayor and the Presidents of Councils—are *ex officio*, and twelve are appointed by the Judges of the Court of Common Pleas. Its meetings are held on the second Wednesday of each month.

It has been determined by the courts of Pennsylvania that any child having lost its father is properly denominated an orphan, irrespective of whether the mother be living or not. This construction has been adopted by the college, the requirements for admission to the institution being prescribed by Mr. Girard's will as follows: (1) The orphan must be a poor white boy, between six and ten years of age, no application for admission being received before the former age, nor can he be admitted into the college after passing his tenth birthday, even though the application has been made previously; (2) the mother or next friend is required to produce the marriage certificate of the child's parents (or, in its absence, some other satisfactory evidence of such marriage), and also the certificate of the physician setting forth the time and place of birth; (3) a form of application looking to the establishment of the child's identity, physical condition, morals, previous education and means of support, must be filled in, signed and vouched for by respectable citizens. Applications are made at the office, No. 19 South Twelfth street, Philadelphia.

A preference is given under Girard's will to (a) orphans born in the city of Philadelphia; (b) those born in any other part of Pennsylvania; (c) those born in the city of New York; (d) those born in the city of New Orleans. The preference to the orphans born in the city of Philadelphia is defined to be strictly limited to the old city proper, the districts subsequently consolidated into the city having no rights in this respect over any other portion of the State.

Orphans are admitted, in the above order, strictly according to priority of application, the mother or next friend executing an indenture binding the orphan to the city of Philadelphia, as trustee under Girard's will, as an orphan to be educated and provided for by the college. The seventh item of the will reads as follows:

"The orphans admitted into the college shall be there fed with plain but wholesome food, clothed with plain but decent apparel (no distinctive dress ever to be worn), and lodged in a plain but safe manner. Due regard shall be paid to their health, and to this end their persons and clothes shall be kept clean, and they shall have suitable and rational exercise and recreation. They shall be instructed in the various branches of a sound education, comprehending reading, writing, grammar, arithmetic, geography, navigation, surveying, practical mathematics, astronomy, natural, chemical, and experimental philosophy, the French and Spanish languages (I do not forbid, but I do not recommend the Greek and Latin languages), and such other learning and science as the capacities of the several scholars may merit or warrant. I would have them taught facts and things, rather than words or signs. And especially, I desire, that by every proper means a pure attachment to our republican institutions, and to the sacred rights of conscience, as guaranteed by our happy constitutions, shall be formed and fostered in the minds of the scholars."

Although the orphans reside permanently in the college, they are, at stated times, allowed to visit their friends at their houses and to receive visits from their friends at the college. The household is under the care of a matron, an assistant matron, prefects and governesses, who superintend the moral and social training of the orphans and administer the discipline of the institution when the scholars are not in the school-rooms. The pupils are divided into sections, for the purposes of discipline, having distinct officers, buildings and playgrounds.

The schools are taught chiefly in the main college building, five professors and forty-eight teachers being employed in the duties of instruction; and the course comprises a thorough English commercial education, to which has been latterly added special schools of technical instruction in the mechanical arts. As a large proportion of the orphans admitted into the college have had little or no preparatory education, the instruction commences with the alphabet.

The order of daily exercises is as follows: the pupils rise at six o'clock; take breakfast at half-past six. Recreation until half-past seven; then assemble in the section rooms at that hour and proceed to the chapel for morning worship at eight. The chapel exercises consist of singing a hymn, reading a chapter from the Old or New Testament, and prayer, after the conclusion of which the pupils proceed to the various school-rooms, where they remain, with a recess of fifteen minutes, until twelve. From twelve until the dinner-hour, which is half-past twelve, they are on the play-ground, returning there after finishing that meal until two o'clock, the afternoon school-hour, when they resume the school exercises, remaining without intermission until four o'clock. At four the afternoon service in the chapel is held, after which they are on the play-ground until six, at which hour supper is served. The evening study hour lasts from seven to eight, or half-past eight, varying with the age of the pupils, the same difference being observed in their bedtimes, which are from half-past seven for the youngest until a quarter before nine for the older boys.

On Sunday the pupils assemble in their section rooms at nine o'clock in the morning and at two in the afternoon for reading and religious instruction, and at half-past ten o'clock in the morning and at three in the afternoon they attend divine worship in the chapel. Here the exercises are similar to those held on week days, with the important addition of an appropriate discourse adapted to the comprehension of the pupils. The services in the chapel, whether on Sundays or on week days, are invariably conducted by the president or other layman, the will of the founder forbidding the entrance of clergymen of any denomination whatsoever within the boundaries of the institution.

The discipline of the college is administered through admonition, deprivation of recreation, and seclusion; but in extreme cases corporal punishment may be inflicted by order of the president and in his presence. If by reason of misconduct a pupil becomes an unfit companion for the rest, the Will says he shall not be permitted to remain in the college.

The annual cost per capita of maintaining, clothing and educating each pupil, including current repairs to buildings and furniture and the maintenance of the grounds, is about three hundred dollars. Between the age of fourteen and eighteen years the scholars may be indentured by the institution, on behalf of "the city of Philadelphia," to learn some "art, trade, or mystery," until their twenty-first year, consulting, as far as is judicious, the inclination and preference of the scholar. The master to whom an apprentice is bound agrees to furnish him with sufficient meat, drink, apparel, washing and lodging at his own place of residence (unless otherwise agreed to by the parties to the indenture and so indorsed upon it); to use his best endeavors to teach and instruct the apprentice in his "art, trade, or mystery," and at the expiration of the apprenticeship to furnish him with at least two complete suits of clothes, one of which shall be new. Should, however, a scholar not be apprenticed by the institution, he must leave the college upon attaining the age of eighteen years. In case of death his friends have the privilege of removing his body for interment, otherwise his remains are placed in the college burial lot at Laurel Hill Cemetery, near Philadelphia.

Citizens and strangers provided with a permit are allowed to visit the college on the afternoon of every week day. Permits can be obtained from the Mayor of Philadelphia, at his office; from a Director; at the office of the Board of City Trusts, No. 19 South Twelfth street, Philadelphia, or at the office of the *Public Ledger* newspaper. Especial courtesy is shown all foreign visitors, and particularly those interested in educational matters.

. . . . . . . . . .

In December, 1831, Mr. Girard was attacked by influenza, which was then epidemic in the city. The violence of the disease greatly prostrated him, and, pneumonia supervening, it became at once apparent that he could not live. He had no fear of death. About a month before this attack he had said: "When Death comes for me he will find me busy, unless I am asleep in bed. If I thought I was going to die to-morrow I should plant a tree, nevertheless, to-day."

He died in the back room of his Water street mansion on December 26th, aged eighty-one years (or nearly), and four days after he was buried in the churchyard at the northwest corner of Sixth and Spruce streets.

For twenty years the remains reposed undisturbed where they had been laid in the churchyard of the Holy Trinity Church; when, the Girard College having been completed, it was resolved that the remains of the donor should be transferred to the marble sarcophagus provided in its vestibule. This was done with appropriate ceremonies on September 30, 1851.

Girard's great ambition was, first, success; and this attained, the longing of mankind to leave a shining memory merged his purpose in the establishment of what was to him that fairest of Utopias—the simple tradition of a citizen. A citizen whose public duties ended not with the State, and whose benefactions were not limited to the rescue or advancement of its interests alone, but whose charities broadened beyond the limits of duty or the boundaries of an individual life, to stretch over long reaches of the future, enriching thousands of poor children in his beloved city yet unborn. His life shows clearly why he worked, as his death showed clearly the fixed object of his labor in acquisition. While he was forward with an apparent disregard of self, to expose his life in behalf of others in the midst of pestilence, to aid the internal improvements of the country, and to promote its commercial prosperity by all the means within his power, he yet had more ambitious designs. He wished to hand himself down to immortality by the only mode that was practicable for a man in his position, and he accomplished precisely that which was the grand aim of his life. He wrote his epitaph in those extensive and magnificent blocks and squares which adorn the streets of his adopted city, in the public works and eleemosynary establishments of his adopted State, and erected his own monument and embodied his own principles in a marble-roofed palace. Yet, splendid as is the structure which stands above his remains, the most perfect model of architecture in the New World, it yields in beauty to the moral monument. The benefactor sleeps among the orphan poor whom his bounty is constantly educating.

"Thus, forever present, unseen but felt, he daily stretches forth his invisible hands to lead some friendless child from ignorance to usefulness. And when, in the fullness of time, many homes have been made happy, many orphans have been fed, clothed and educated, and many men made useful to their country and themselves, each happy home or rescued child or useful citizen will be a living monument to perpetuate the name and embalm the memory of the 'Mariner and Merchant.'"

# BOARD OF DIRECTORS
## OF
# CITY TRUSTS,
## 1908.

LOUIS WAGNER, *President*,
*Ex-Officio Member of all Standing Committees.*

JOHN H. CONVERSE, *Vice-President.*

| | |
|---|---|
| FRANCIS SHUNK BROWN, | ALFRED MOORE, |
| JOHN M. CAMPBELL, | CHARLES E. MORGAN, |
| JOHN K. CUMING, | WILLIAM POTTER, |
| SAMUEL DICKSON, | EDWARD B. SMITH, |
| WILLIAM H. LAMBERT, | EDWIN S. STUART. |

MEMBERS OF THE BOARD "EX OFFICIO:"

JOHN E. REYBURN, *Mayor.*
JAMES M. HAZLETT, *President of Select Council.*
GEORGE McCURDY, *President of Common Council.*

FRANK M. HIGHLEY, *Secretary.*
FRANCIS E. BREWSTER, *Solicitor.*
JOHN S. BOYD, *Supt. of Admission and Indentures.*

B. B. COMEGYS.

# HOW TO WIN SUCCESS.

May 27, 1888.

I WISH to speak to you to-day about some of the plainest duties of life—of what you must be, of what you must do, if you would be good men and succeed.

It would be strange if one who has lived as long as I have should not have learned something worth knowing and worth telling to those who are younger and less experienced. I have had much to do with young people here and elsewhere, and I have seen many failures, much disappointment, many wrecks of character, and have learned many things; and I speak to you to-day in the hope that I may say such things as will help some boy, at least one, to determine, while he is here this morning, to do the best he can, each for himself, as well as for others. My remarks are particularly appropriate to those just about to leave the college.

It is convenient for me to consider the whole subject—

1. As to health.
2. As to improvement of the mind.
3. As to business or work of any kind.

4. As to your duties to other people.

5. As to your duty to God.

1. As to health. You cannot be happy without good health, and you cannot expect to have good health unless you observe certain conditions. You must keep your person cleanly by bathing, when that is within reach, or by other simple methods (such as a common brush) which are always within your reach. Be as much in the open air as possible. This is, of course, to those whose work is within doors and sedentary, such as that of a clerk in any shop or office. Pure, fresh air is Nature's own provision for the well-being of all her creatures, and is the best of all tonics.

Be careful of your diet; for it is not good to eat food that is too highly seasoned or too rich. Don't be afraid of fruit in season and when it is ripe. But don't eat much late at night. Late hot suppers are apt to do great harm. The plain, wholesome food provided here, accounts for the extraordinarily good health which almost all of you enjoy.

Have nothing whatever to do with intoxicating drinks. And the only way to be absolutely safe is not to drink even a little, or once in a while. Don't drink at all.

Be sure you get plenty of sleep. Be in bed not later than eleven o'clock, and, better still, at ten. A young fellow who goes to work at seven o'clock in the morning can't afford to keep late hours. Young people need more sleep than older ones, and you cannot safely disregard this hint. Late hours are always more or less injurious, especially when you are away from home or in the streets. Beware of the temptations of the streets and at the theatres.

As to public entertainments or recreations in the evening, go to no place of seeing or hearing where you would not be willing to take your mother or sister. If you keep to this rule you are not likely to be hurt. If you play games, avoid billiard saloons, and gambling houses, or parties. You cannot be too careful about your recreations; let them be simple and healthful as to mind and body, and cheap.

Have no personal habits, such as smoking, or chewing, or spitting, or swearing, or others that are injurious to yourselves or disagreeable to other people. All these are either injurious or disagreeable. Have clean hands and clean clothes, not while you are at work—this is not always possible—but when going and coming to and from work.

Always give place to women in the streets, in street-cars, or in other places. Do not rush into street-cars first to get seats. A true gentleman will wait until women get in before he goes. Do not sit in street-cars, while women are standing, unless you are very, very tired. Here is a temptation before you every day almost in our city. Hardly anything is more trying than to see sturdy boys sitting in cars while women are standing and holding on to straps.

And yet I see this every day. What is a boy good for, that will not stand for a few minutes, if he can give a woman or an old man a seat?

If you are so favored as to have a few days or two weeks holiday in summer, go to the country or to the sea-shore, if your means will allow. The country air or sea air is better for you than almost any other change.

Do not be extravagant in dress; but be well dressed—not, however, at your tailor's expense. It is the duty of all to be well dressed, but don't spend all your money on dress, and especially don't buy clothing on credit. It is particularly trying to pay for clothing when it is nearly or quite worn out. By all means keep out of debt, for your personal or family expenses, unless you are sure beyond any doubt that you can very soon repay your dealer the money you owe. The difference between ease and comfort, and distress, in money matters, is whether you spend a little more than you make, or a little less than you make. Don't forget the "rainy day" that is pretty sure to come, and you must lay up something for that day.

Very much of the crime that is committed every day (and you cannot open a paper without seeing an account of some one who has gone wrong) is because people will live beyond their means; will spend more than they earn. They hope for an increase of pay, or that they will make money in some way or other, and then when that good time does not come, and as they can't afford to wait for it, they take something, only borrowing it as they say, but they take it and spend it, or pay some pressing debt with it, and then, and then—they are caught, and sent to court, and tried and sent to—well, you know without my telling you.

As to the mind.

You have fine opportunities for education here, but they will soon be over, and if you leave this college without having a good knowledge of the practical branches of study pursued here, and which Mr. Girard especially enjoined should be taught, you will be at a great disadvantage with other boys who are well educated. I had a letter in my pocket a few days ago written by a Girard boy, and dated in the Moyamensing Prison, full of bad spelling and bad grammar; and next to the horror of knowing he was in prison, I felt ashamed, that a boy so ignorant of the very commonest branches of English education should have ever been within the walls of this college.

I think I have told you before of a man who employs a large number of men, whose business amounts to perhaps hundreds of thousands of dollars in a year, who is entirely ignorant of accounts, and who a few years ago was robbed and almost ruined by his book-keeper, and who would now give half of what he is worth, and that is a good deal, if he could understand book-keeping; for he is entirely dependent upon other people to keep his accounts.

As to books, be careful what you read. How it grieves me to see errand boys in street-cars, and sometimes as they walk in the streets, reading such stuff as is found in the dime novels. Not merely a waste of time, though that is bad enough, but a positive injury to the mind, filling it with the most improbable stories, and often, also, with that which is positively vicious. Read something better than this. Do not confine yourselves to newspapers, and do not read police reports. Attractive as this class of reading is, it is for the most part hurtful to the young mind. There is an abundance of cheap and good reading, magazines and periodicals; and books and books, good, bad, indifferent; and you will hardly know which to choose unless you ask others who are older than you, and who know books. Most boys read little but novels; and there are many thoroughly good novels, humorous, and pathetic, and historical. Don't buy books unless you have plenty of money; for you can get everything you want out of the public libraries; and this was not so, or at least to this extent, when I was a boy.

As to work or business.

Set out with the determination that you will be faithful in everything. Only last week a Girard boy called on me to help him get employment. I asked him some questions, and he told me that he had been out of the college five or six years, and had five or six situations. Do you think he had been faithful in anything? If he had been, he would not have lost place after place. When you get a place, and I hope every one of you will have a place provided for you before you leave here, be among the first to arrive in the morning, and be among the last to leave at the end of the day's work. Do not let any fascination of base ball or anything else lead you to forget that your first duty is to your employer. Be quick to answer every call. Don't say to yourself, "It is not my place to answer that call, it is the other boy's place," but go yourself, if the other fellow is slow, and let it be seen that you are ready for any work. And be very prompt to answer. Do whatever you are told. Say "yes, sir," "no, sir" with hearty good-will, and say "good-morning" as if you meant it. In short, do not be slovenly in anything you have to do; be alive, and remember all the time that no labor is degrading.

Be sure to treat your employers with unfailing respect, and your fellow-clerks or workers, whether superiors, inferiors or equals, with hearty good-will.

Do not tell lies directly or indirectly, for even if your employer do so, he will despise you for doing so. No matter if he is untruthful, he will respect you if you tell the truth always. Do not indulge in or listen to impure talk. No real gentleman does this, and you can be a real gentleman even if you are poor, for you will be educated. Make yourself indispensable to your employer; this, too, is quite possible, and it will almost certainly insure success. Be ambitious in the highest sense. Remember, that if not now, you will hereafter have others dependent upon you for support or help. It is a splendid thing for a boy to go out from this college with the determination to support his mother; and some that I know and you know are doing this, and many others will do it.

I pause here to say that, so far, my words have been spoken as to your duties to the world, to yourselves. I have supposed that you boys would rather be bosses than journeymen, that you would rather own teams than drive them for other people, that you would rather be a contractor than carry the pick and shovel, that you would rather be a bricklayer than carry the hod, that you would rather be a house-builder than a shoveler of coal into the house-builder's cellar. Is it not so?

Now, I say that if you should do everything I tell you, and avoid everything I have warned you against, you cannot succeed in the best sense, you cannot become true men, such men as the city has a right to expect you to be, unless you seek the blessing of God; for he holds all things in his hands. "The silver and the gold are mine, and the cattle upon a thousand hills." If God be for us, who can be against us?

In these closing words, then, I would speak to you as to your duty to God.

What shall I say about this? I can hardly tell you anything that you do not already know, so often have you been talked to about this subject. But nothing is so important for you to be reminded of, though I fear that to some of you hardly anything is so uninteresting. Naturally the heart is disinclined to think of God and our duty to him. But we cannot do without him, though many people think they can, or they act as if they thought so. Such people are not wise; they are very foolish.

He made us, he preserves us, he cares for us with infinite love and care, he has appointed the time for our departure from this life, and he has prepared a better life than this for those who love him here. We cannot afford to disregard such a being as this, for all things are in his hands. If you will think of it, some of the best men and women you know are believers in God, and are trying to serve him. Do you think you can do without him?

Cultivate, then, the companionship, the friendship of those who love and fear God, both men and women. You are safe with such; you are not quite so sure of safety in the society of those who openly say they can do without God. When I speak of those who fear God, I do not mean merely professors of religion, not merely members of meeting or members of church, but I mean people who live such lives as people ought to live, who fear God and keep his commandments. You know there are such, you have met with them, you will meet many more of them, and you will meet also those who call themselves Christians, but whose lives show that they have no true knowledge of God, who are mere formalists, mere professors.

Become acquainted with your Bible. I mean, read it, a little of it at least, every day. You need not read much, it is well sometimes that you read but a little; but read it with a purpose—that is, to understand it. The literature of the Bible as you grow older will abundantly repay your careful and constant reading even before you reach its spiritual treasuries. In reading a few days ago the argument of Horace Binney, Esq., in the Girard will case, I was surprised to see how familiar Mr. Binney was with the Bible, and he was one of the ablest lawyers that has ever lived in our own or any other country. Yet Mr. Binney thought it quite worth his while to read and study the Bible. Don't you think it is worth your while also?

Be a regular attendant at some church. I do not say what church it shall be. That must be left to yourselves to determine, and many circumstances will arise to aid you in your choice. But let it be some church, and, when you become more interested in the subject than you are now, join that church, whatever it may be, and so connect yourselves with people who believe in and love God. If there be a Bible class there, connect yourselves with it, and so learn to study the Scriptures systematically.

Do not be ashamed to kneel at your bedside every night and every morning and pray to God. You are not so likely to be ashamed if you have a room to yourself; but you must not be ashamed to do this even if there are others in the room with you, as will be the case with many of you. This is a severe test, I know, but he who bears it faithfully will already have gained a victory.

Commit to memory the fifteenth verse of the twelfth chapter of the Gospel according to St. Luke: "Take heed and beware of covetousness, for a man's life consisteth not in the abundance of the things he possesseth."

On last Monday, Founder's Day, there were gathered here many men, a great company, who were trained in this college, and who, after graduation, went out into the world to seek their fortune. It is always a most interesting time, not only for them but for the teachers and officers who have had charge of them.

Some of them are successful men in the highest and best sense, and have made themselves a name and a place in the world. Bright young lawyers, clerks, mechanics, railroad men—men representing almost all kinds of business and occupations—came here in great numbers to celebrate the anniversary of the birth of the Founder of this great school. It was a grand sight. Hardly anything impresses me more. I do not know their names; for many of them had left before I began to come here; but from certain expressions that fell from the lips of some of them I am persuaded that they, at least, are walking in the truth.

It would be very interesting if we could know their thoughts, and see with what feelings they look back on their school-life. I wonder if any of them regret that they did not make a better use of their time while here. I wonder if any feel that they would like to become boys again and go to school over again, being sure that, with their present experience of life, they would set a higher value on the education of the schools. I wonder if any feel that they would have reached higher positions and secured a larger influence if they had been more diligent at school. I wonder if there are any who can trace evil habits of thought to the companions they had here. I wonder if any are aware of evil impressions which they made on their classmates and so cast a stain and a dark shadow on other young lives, stains never obliterated, shadows never wholly lifted. I wonder if there are any among them who regret that the opportunity of seeking God and finding God in their school-days was neglected, and who have never had so favorable an opportunity since. "If some who come back here on these commemoration days were to tell you all their thoughts on such subjects, they would be eloquent with a peculiar eloquence."

I wish I could persuade you, especially you larger boys, to give most earnest attention to the duties which lie before you every day. You will not misunderstand me, nor be so unjust to me as to suppose that I would interfere in the least degree with the pleasures which belong to your time of life. I would not lessen them in the least; on the contrary, I would encourage you, and help you in all proper recreation, in all sports and plays. The boy who does not enjoy play is not a happy boy, and is not very likely to make a happy man, or a useful man. But it is quite possible, as some of you know, to enjoy in the highest degree all healthful sports, and at the same time to be industrious and conscientious in your studies. I am deeply concerned that the boys in this college shall be boys of the best, the highest type; that they "shall walk in the truth." There are, alas, many boys who have gone through this college, and fully equipped (as well as their teachers could equip them), have been launched out into life and come to naught. I do not know their names nor do you, probably, though you do not doubt the fact.

Whatever others say, who speak to you here, I want to discharge my duty to you as faithfully as I can. I know some of the difficulties of life, for they have been in my path. I know some of the fierce temptations to which boys and young men are exposed, for I have felt these assaults in my own person. I know what it is to sin against God, for I am a sinner; so, with my sympathies quick towards you, I come with these plain, earnest words, and I urge you to look up to God, and ask him to help you. He can help you, and he will, if you ask him.

# LIFE—ITS OPPORTUNITIES AND TEMPTA- TIONS.

March 12, 1885.

I PROPOSE to speak to you now of some plain and practical duties which await you in life; and, as there are many boys here who are anxiously looking for the time when they will leave the college to make their way in the world, some of whom will probably have left the college before I come again, I speak more especially to them. And my first words are words of congratulation, and for these reasons:

1. *Because you are young.* And this means very much. You have an enormous advantage over people that are your seniors. Other things being equal, you will live longer, and I assume that "life is worth living." Then you have the advantage of profiting by the mistakes committed by those who precede you, and if you are not blind, you can avail yourselves of the successes they have achieved.

You have the freshness, the zest of youth. You are full of courage and endurance. You can grapple with difficult subjects and with a strong hand. And if you blunder, you have time to recover yourselves and start anew. In short, life is before you, and you look forward with the inspiration of hope, and it may be, also, of determination.

2. I congratulate you also *because you are poor*. You have your own way to make in the world. You know already that if you achieve success, it must be because you exert yourselves to the very utmost. Indeed, you must depend upon yourselves, and this means that you must do everything in your power that is right to do, to help yourselves.

You must understand that there is no royal road to *success*, any more than there is to *learning*, and that there is no time to trifle. If you were rich men's sons, these remarks would have no special pertinence, or importance.

My congratulations are quite in order also because very many, if not *most* of the high places in our country, are held by those who once were poor lads.

Should you turn upon me and say, "Why, then, if one is to be congratulated on his poverty, do fathers toil early and late, denying themselves needed recreation, not ceasing when they have accumulated a good estate, almost selling their souls to become millionaires—why do they so much dread to leave their sons to struggle for a living?" More than one answer might be given to these questions. Some fathers have so little faith in God's providence that they forget his goodness, which *now* takes care of their families through the instrumentality of parents;

and who can continue that care through other means, just as well, when the parents are gone; but high authority says that "they who will be rich, fall into temptations and snares," one of which is that the race for riches unfits the racer for all other pursuits and amusements, and he can't stop his course, he can't change his habits, he has no other mental resources—he must work or perish.

Do not, then, let the fact that you are *poor* discourage you in the least—it is rather an advantage.

3. But again I congratulate you, because *your lot is cast in America.* Do not smile at this. I am not on the point of flying the American eagle, nor of raising the stars and stripes. It *is*, however, a good thing to have been born in this country. For in all important respects it is the most favored of all lands. It is the fashion with certain people to disparage our government and its institutions; and one must admit that in some particulars there might be improvement, and will be some day; but, notwithstanding these defects, it is unquestionably true that it is the best government on earth. Is there any country where a poor young man has opportunities as good as he has here, to get on in life? Is there any obstacle or hindrance whatever, outside of himself, in the way of his success? If a young man has good health of mind and body, and a fair English education and good manners, and will be honest and industrious, is he not much more certain to attain success, in one

way or another, in this country than anywhere else? You know he is. Why? Because of our equal rights under the law. There is no caste here, that curse of monarchies. There is no aristocracy in sentiment or in power, no House of Lords, no established church, no law of primogeniture. One man is as good as another under the law as long as he behaves himself.

If you want further evidence, only look for a moment at the condition of the seething, surging masses of Europe, and the continual apprehensions of a general war. Before this year 1885 has run its course the United States may be almost the only country among the great powers that is not involved in war.

And if still further illustration were needed, let me point to that most extraordinary scene enacted in Washington some weeks ago.

A great political party, which has held control of this government nearly a quarter of a century, and which has exercised almost unlimited power, yields most quietly and gracefully all high places, all dignity, all honor and patronage, to the will of the people who have chosen a new administration. And everybody regards it as a matter of course.

Was such a thing ever known before? And could such a thing occur anywhere else among the nations?

Once more, I congratulate you *because you live in Philadelphia*. Ah, now we come to a most interesting point. Most of you were born here, and you come to this by inheritance. This is the best of all large cities. More to be desired as a place to live in than Washington, the seat of government, the most beautiful of all American cities, or New York, with its vast commerce and enormous wealth, or Boston, with its boasted intellectual society.

They may call us the "*Quaker City*," or the "*worst paved city*," or the "*slow city*," or the " city of rows of houses exactly alike;" but these houses are the homes of separate families, and in a very large degree are occupied by their owners, and you cannot say as much of any other city in the world. Although there are doubtless many instances in the oldest part of the city, and among the improvident poor, where more than one family will be found in the same house, yet these are the exceptions and not the rule; and so far as I know there is not one " tenement house" in this great city that was built for the purpose of accommodating several families at the same time. I need not point you to New York and Boston, where the great apartment houses, with their twelve and fourteen stories of flats for rich and well-to-do people prevail, utterly destroying that most cherished domestic life of which we have been so proud, and introducing the life of European cities, with its demoralizing associations and results; nor shall I describe the awful tenement houses in those two cities, where the poor are crowded like animals in a cattle-train, suffering as the poor dumb creatures do, for want of air, and water, and space, and everything else that makes life desirable.

Of all cities on the face of the earth, Philadelphia is the most desirable for the young man who must make his own way in the world. . . .

And having shown you how favorable are the conditions which are about you, the next point is, What will you do when you set out for yourselves?

All of you are *expecting* when you leave school to be employed by somebody, or engaged in some business. And I suppose you may be looking to me to give you some hints how to take care of yourselves, or how to behave in such relations.

I will try to do so plainly and faithfully.

I cannot absolutely promise you success. Indeed, it would be necessary first to define the word. And there are several definitions that might be given. One of the shortest and best would be in these words, "A life well spent." That's success. And this definition shall be my model.

Work hard, then, at your lessons. Let your ambition be, not to get through quickly, not to go over much ground in text-books, but to master thoroughly everything before you. If you knew how little thorough instruction there is, you would thank me for this. There are so many half-educated people from schools and colleges that one cannot help believing that the terms of graduation are very easy. There have been, and are now, graduates of colleges who cannot add up a long column of figures correctly, nor do an example in simple proportion, nor write a letter of four pages of note paper without mistakes of grammar and spelling and punctuation, to say nothing of perspicuity and unity and general good taste.

It is quite surprising to find how helpless some young men are in the simple matter of writing letters; an art with which, in these days of cheap postage and cheap stationery, almost everybody has something to do. If you doubt this let me ask you to try to-morrow to write a note of twenty lines on any subject whatever, off-hand, and submit it for criticism to your teacher. Do you wonder, then, that an employer calling one of his young men, and directing him to write a letter to one of his correspondents, saying such and such things, and bring it to him for his signature, is surprised and grieved to see that the letter is in such shape that he cannot sign it and let it go out of his office?

It is very true that letter-writing is not the chief business of life, not the only thing of importance in a counting-house, but it is an elegant accomplishment, and most desirable of attainment.

Let me say some words about shorthand writing. In this day of push and drive and hurry, when so many things must be done at once, there is an increasing demand for shorthand writers. In fact, business as now conducted cannot afford to do without this help. It often occurs that a principal in a business house cannot take the time to write long letters. Why should he? It does not pay to have one that is occupied in governing and controlling great interests, or in the receipt of a large salary, tied to a desk writing letters, or reports, or statements of any kind. He must *talk off* these things; and he must be an educated man, whose mind is so disciplined to terse and accurate expression that his dictation may almost be taken to be final. He wants a clerk who can take down his words with literal accuracy, and who will be able to correct any errors that may have been spoken, and submit the complete paper to his chief for his signature. The demand for this kind of service is increasing every day, and some of you now listening to me will be so employed. See that you are ready for it when your opportunity comes.

If you get to be a clerk in a railroad office, or in an insurance company, or in a store, or in a bank, devote yourself to your particular duties, whatever they may be. And don't be too particular as to what kind of work it is that falls to your lot. It may be work that you think belongs to the porter; no matter if it is, do it, and do it as well as the porter can, or even better.

Let none of you, therefore, think that anything you are likely to be called upon to do is beneath you. Do it, and do it in the best manner, and you may not have to do it for a long time.

Make yourself indispensable to your employer. You can do that; it is quite within your power, and it may be that you may get to be an employer yourself; indeed it is more than probable; but you must work for it.

If you get to be a bookkeeper in any counting-house or public institution, remember that you are in a position of trust and responsibility. When you make errors do not erase the error; draw faint red or black lines through it and write correct characters over the error. Do not hide your errors of any kind. Do not misstate anything in language or figures. Everybody makes errors at some time or other, but everybody does not admit and apologize for them. The honest man is he who *does* admit and apologize, and does so without waiting to be detected.

There have been of late some deplorable instances of betrayal of trust in our city. I may as well call it by its right name, stealing. The culprits are now suffering in prison the penalty for their crimes. While I am speaking to you there are men, young and *not* young, in our city who are *now* stealing, and who are falsifying their books in the vain hope that it may be kept secret; who are dreading the day when they will be caught; who cannot afford to take a holiday; who cannot afford to be sick, lest absence for a single day may disclose their guilt. What a horrible state of mind! They will go to their desks or their offices to-morrow morning, not knowing but it may be their last day in that place.

And the day will come, most surely, when *you* will be tempted as these wretched ones have been tempted. In what shape the temptation may come, or when, no human being knows. The suggestion will be made, that by the use of a little money you may make a good deal; that the venture is perfectly safe; some one tells you so, and points to this one or that one who has tried it and made money. It is only a little thing; you can't lose much; you *may* make enough to pay for the cost of your summer holiday, or for your cigar bill, or your beer bill; or you will be able to smoke better cigars or drink better beer, or buy a gold watch, or a diamond ring, or anything else; *you can't lose much.* You have no money of your own, it is true, but what is needed will not be missed if you take it out of the drawer. Shall you do it? No! Let nothing induce you to take the first dollar not your own. It is the *first* step that counts.

But suppose you don't care for this warning, or forget it. Suppose the time comes when you find that you *have* taken something that was not yours, and that it is lost, and that you cannot repay it, what then? Why, go at once to your employer; tell him the whole story; keep back nothing; throw yourself upon his mercy, and ask forgiveness. Better now than later. You will assuredly be caught. There is no possibility of continuous concealment. Tell it now before you are detected, and, if you must be disgraced, the sooner the better.

Am I too earnest about this? Am I saying too much? Oh, boys, young men, if you knew the frightful danger that you may be in some day, the subtle temptations that will beset you, the many instances of weakness about you, the shipwrecks of character, the utter ruin that comes to sisters and to innocent wives and children by the crimes of brothers, husbands and fathers, as we who are older know, you would not wonder that I speak as I do.

Every case of breach of trust, every defalcation, weakens confidence in human character. For every such instance of wrong-doing is a stab at *your* integrity if you are in a position of trust. Men of the fairest reputation, men who are trusted implicitly by their employers, men who are hedged about by the sacredness of domestic ties, on whom the happiness of helpless wives and innocent children depend, men who claim to be religious, go astray, step by step, little by little; they defraud, steal, lie, try to cover up their tracks, cannot do it long, are caught, tried, convicted, sentenced and imprisoned. Then the question may be asked about you or me: "How do we know that Mr. So-and-So is any better than those who have fallen?" Don't you see that these culprits are enemies of the public confidence, enemies of society, *your* enemies and *mine?*

If the names of those who are now serving out

their sentences in the public prisons for stealing, not petty theft, but stealing and defrauding in larger sums, could be published in to-morrow morning's papers, what a sad record it would be of dishonored names and blighted lives and ruined homes, and how the memory would recall some whom we knew in early youth, the pride of their parents, or the idol of fond wives and lovely children; and we should turn away with sickening horror from the record! But, if there should appear in the same papers the names of those who are *now engaged in stealing and defrauding* and *falsifying entries,* who are not yet caught, but who may, before this year is out, be caught and convicted and punished, what a horrible revelation *that* would be!

. . . . . . . . .

I close abruptly, for I cannot keep you longer.

But do not think that it is for your future in *this* life only that I am concerned. Life does not end here, though it may seem to do so. Our life in this world is a mere *beginning* of existence. It is the *future,* the *endless* life before us, that we should prepare for; and no preparation is worth the name except that of a pure, an upright and honorable life, that depends for its support on the love and the fear of God. You must accept him as your Father, you must honor him and obey him, and so consecrating your young lives to his service, trust him to care for you with his infinite love and care.

# ON THE DEATH OF WILLIAM WELSH,
*First President of the Board of City Trusts.*

February 22, 1878.

WHEN I spoke to you last from this desk I tried to persuade you to adopt the thought so aptly set forth by one of the old Hebrew kings, Whatsoever thy hand findeth to do, do it with thy might. I little thought then that Mr. Welsh, who was one of the most conspicuous examples of working with all his might, and so much of whose work was done for you, whom you so often saw standing where I now stand, I little thought that his work on earth was so nearly done. Last Sunday he addressed you here. One, two, three services he conducted for the boys of this college, one in the infirmary, one in the refectory for the new boys, and one in this chapel. I venture to say from my knowledge of his method of doing things that these services were all conducted in the best manner possible to him; that he did not spare his strength; that there was nothing weak or undecided in his acts or speech, but that he took hold of his subject with a firm grasp, and did not let go until the service was finished. It is very natural that we should desire to know as much as we can about a life that has come so close to us as the life of Mr. Welsh, and to learn, if we may, what it was that made him the man that he was. The thousands of people that gathered in and about St. Luke's Church on the day of the funeral, as many of you saw; the very large number of citizens of the highest distinction who united in the solemn services; the profound interest manifested everywhere among all classes of society; the closing of places of business at the hour of these services; the flags at half-mast, all these circumstances, so unusual, so impressive, assured us that no common man had gone from among us. What was it that made him no common man? What was there in his life and character that lifted him above the ordinarily successful merchant? In other places, and by those most competent to speak, will the complete picture of his life be drawn, but what was there in his life which particularly interests you college boys? It will surprise you probably when I tell you that his early education—the education of the schools—was very limited. He was not a college-bred man. At a very early age (as early as fourteen, I believe) he left school and went into his father's store. You know that he could not have had much education at that age. And he went into the store, not to be a gentleman clerk to sit in the counting-house and copy letters and invoices, and do the bank business and lounge about in fine clothing, but he went to do anything that came to hand, rough and smooth, hard and easy, dirty and clean, for in those days the duties of a junior clerk differed from those of a porter only in this, that the young clerk's work was not so heavy as the robust porter's. And even when he grew older and stronger he would go down into the hold of a vessel and vie with the strong stevedore in the shifting and placing of cargoes. And the days were long then: there were no office hours from nine to three o'clock, but merchants and their clerks dined near the middle of the day, and were back at their stores, their warehouses, in the afternoon and stayed and worked until the day was done. So this young clerk worked all day, and went home at night tired and hungry, to rest, to sleep and to go through the next day and the next in the same manner. But not only to rest and sleep. The body was tired enough with the long day's work, but the mind was not tired. He early knew the importance of mental discipline, of mental cultivation. He knew that a half-educated man is no match for one thoroughly equipped, and so he set himself to the task of making up, as far as he could, for that deficiency of systematic education which his early withdrawal from school made him regret so much. What definite means or methods he resorted to to accomplish this I cannot tell you, for I have not learned; but the fact that he did very largely overcome this most serious disadvantage is apparent to all who have ever met him. He was a cultivated gentleman, thoroughly at ease in circles where men must be well informed or be very uncomfortable. As the President of this Board of Trustees, having for his associates gentlemen of the highest professional and general culture, he was quite equal to any exigency which ever arose. All this you must know was the result of education, not that which was imparted to him in the schools, but that which he acquired himself after his school life. He was careful about his associates. Then, as now, the streets were alive with boys and young men of more than questionable character. And the thought which has come up in many a boy's mind after his day's work was done, must have come up in his mind: "Why should I not stroll about the streets with companions of my own age and have a good time? Why should I be so strict while others have more freedom and enjoy themselves so much more?" I have no doubt that he had his enjoyments, and that he was a free, hearty boy in them all, but I cannot suppose, for his after life gave no evidence of it, his general good health, his muscular wiry frame forbade the thought, I cannot suppose his youthful pleasures passed beyond that line which separates the good from the bad, the pure from the impure. Few evils are so great as that of evil companions.

William Welsh was not afraid of work. I mean by that he was not lazy. A large part of the failures in life are attributable to the love of ease. We choose the soft things; we turn away from those which are hard. We are deterred by the abstruse, the obscure; we are attracted by the simple, the plain. A really strong character will grapple with any subject; a weak one shrinks from a struggle. A character naturally weak may be developed by culture and discipline into one of real strength, but the process is very slow and very discouraging. A life that is worth anything at all, that impresses itself on other lives, on society, must have these struggles, this training. I do not know minutely the characteristics of Mr. Welsh's early life in this particular, but I infer most emphatically that his strong character was formed by continuous, laborious, exacting self-application.

I would now speak of that quality which is so valuable (I will not say so rare), so conspicuously and so immeasurably important, personal integrity. Mr. Welsh possessed this in the highest degree. He was most emphatically an honest man. No thought of anything other than this could ever have entered into the mind of any one who knew him. All men knew that public or private trusts committed to him were safe. Mistakes in judgment all are liable to, but of conscious deflection from the right path in this respect he was incapable. His high position as President of the Board of City Trusts, which includes, among other large properties, the great estate left by Mr. Girard to the city of Philadelphia, proves the confidence this community had in his personal character. His private fortune was used as if he were a trustee. He recognized the hand of God in his grand success as a merchant, and he felt himself accountable to God for a proper expenditure. If he enjoyed a generous mode of living for himself and his family—a manner of life required by his position in the community—he more than equalized it by his gifts to objects of benevolence. He was conscientious and liberal (rare combination) in his benefactions, for he felt that he held his personal property in trust.

Such are a few of the traits in the character of the man whose life on earth was so suddenly closed on Monday last. Under Providence, by which I mean the blessing of God, that blessing which is just as much within your reach as his, these are some of the conditions of his extraordinary success. His self-culture, the choice of his companions his persistent industry, his integrity, his religion, made the man what he was. I cannot here speak of his work in that church which he loved so much. I do not speak with absolute certainty, but I have reason to believe that, next to his own family, his affections were placed on you. He could never look into your faces without having his feelings stirred to their profoundest depths. He loved you—in the best, the truest sense, he loved you. He was willing to give any amount of his time, his thought, his care, to you. The time he spent in the chapel was a very small part of the time he gave to his work for you. You were upon his heart constantly. I do not know —no one can know—but if it be possible for the spirits of just men made perfect to revisit the scenes of earth —to come back and look upon those they loved so much when in the flesh—I am sure his spirit is here to-day—this, his first Sabbath in Heaven—looking into your faces, as he often did when he went in and out among you, and wishing that all of you may make such use of your grand opportunity here as will insure your success in the life which is before you when you leave these college walls, and especially as will insure your entering into the everlasting life. Such was his life, full of activity, generosity, self-denial, eminently religious, in the best sense successful. He was never at rest; his heart was always open to human sympathy; he denied nothing except to himself. He wanted everybody to be religious. He died in the harness; no time to take it off; no wish to take it off. But in the front, on the advance, not in retreat. He never turned his back on anything that was right. His eye was not dim; his natural force was not abated. Death came so swiftly that it seemed only stepping from one room in his Father's house to another. We are reminded of the beautiful words in which Mr. Thackeray describes the death of Colonel Newcome in the hospital of the Charter House School, after a life spent in fighting the enemies of his country abroad, and the enemies of the good in society at home. "At the usual evening hour the chapel bell began to toll and Thomas Newcome's hands outside the bed feebly beat time. And just as the last bell struck, a peculiar sweet smile shone over his face. He lifted up his head a little and quickly said *Adsum*, and fell back. It was the word they used at school when names were called, and lo, he, whose heart was as that of a little child, had answered to his name and stood in the presence of 'The Master.'"

## BAD ASSOCIATES.

November 11, 1888.

I WISH to speak to you to-day about the danger of evil company, a danger to which you will necessarily be exposed when you go out from this college to make your way in life.

The desire for companionship sometimes leads people, and especially young people, into bad company. A boy finds himself associated with a schoolmate, a fellow-apprentice or fellow-clerk, who is attractive in manners, full of fun, but who is not what he ought to be in character.

No one is entirely bad; almost all persons old or young have some points that are not repulsive, and sometimes the very bad are attractive in some respects. A comparatively innocent boy is thrown into such company, and, at first, he sees nothing in the conduct of his new friends which is particularly out of the way. The conversation is somewhat guarded, the jokes and stories are not specially bad, and, for a time, nothing occurs to shock his feelings; but, after a while, the mask is thrown off and the true character is revealed. Then very soon the mind of the pure, innocent boy receives impressions that corrupt and defile it. All that is polluting in talk and story and song is poured out. Books and papers, so vile that it is a breach of law to sell them, are read and quoted without bringing a blush to the cheek, and, before his parents are aware of the danger, the mind and heart of their son are so polluted and depraved that no human power can save him.

I very well remember a boy older than myself who, early in life, gave himself up to vile company and vile books and vile habits, and who, long ago—almost as soon as he reached an early manhood—sunk, under the weight of his sinful habits, into a dishonored grave, but not until he had defiled and depraved many a boy who came under his influence. Better would it have been for his companions if their daily walks and playgrounds had been infested with venomous serpents, to bite and sting their bare feet, than to associate with a boy whose heart was full of all uncleanness.

It is dangerous to make such friendships. Circumstances may throw us among them; the providence of God may send us there, but we ought never to *seek* such company, except for good purposes. What I mean is that we ought not to seek such associates, however agreeable they may be in other respects, and not to remain among them except for their good.

There are wicked people in every community,

all ages. We cannot altogether avoid contact with them. We find them among our schoolmates and in the walks of business.

Many a young man, many a boy, has been forever ruined by evil companions. A corrupt literature is bad enough, but evil companions are more numerous and, if possible, more fatal. Bad books and papers have slain their thousands; bad companions have slain their ten thousands. I can recall the names of many who were led away, step by step, down the broad road that leads to destruction, by companions genial, attractive, but corrupt.

There are some companions from whom you cannot separate yourselves. They are with you continually; at home and abroad, in school or at play, by day and by night, asleep and awake, they are always with you. There is no solitude so deep that they cannot find you, no crowd so great that they will ever lose you. No matter who else is with you, they will not—cannot—be kept away. I mean *your own thoughts*, your bosom companions. Shall they be EVIL companions or GOOD? Ah! you know who, and who only, can answer this question.

I once went through a monastery in the old city of Florence, in Italy. It was a retreat for men who were tired of the world, or who felt so unequal to the strife and conflict of life in the world that they believed peace could be found only in retirement. The house was of the order of St. Francis. One of the monks took me into his cell, and I sat down and talked with him. It was a very small room—one door, one window, bare walls, a small table, two wooden chairs, a few books, a crucifix, a washstand, and some pieces of crockery; and that was all. In this room he lived, never to leave it except to go to the chapel, just across the corridor, and to walk in the cloisters for exercise; here he expected to die. It seemed very dreary and lonely to me. But I thought, if this were a certain and sure way of escaping from evil thoughts, and the only way, men may well submit to the confinement, the solitude, the monotony, the dreariness of this way of life. But, alas! it is not so. No close and narrow cell, no iron doors, no bolts and bars, can shut out our thoughts, for they are a part of ourselves: they *are* ourselves; for, "as a man thinketh in his heart, so is he."

Some years ago a country lad left his home to seek his fortune in the city. His mother was dead and his father broken in health and in fortune. The boy reached the city full of high hopes, promising his father that he would do his best to succeed in whatever fell to his lot to do. He was tall, strong and good-looking. A place was soon found for him, and until he was better able to support himself he found a home with some friends. He was a boy of good mind but with a very imperfect education, and he seemed inclined to make up for this in part by reading during his leisure hours. The situation found for him was in a large commercial house, where everything was conducted in the best manner and on the highest principles. Here he made rapid progress and was soon able to contribute to the support of those he had left at home in the country. He became interested in serious things, united with the Sunday-school, and after a while made a profession of religion. Everything went well with him for several years, until he fell in with some boys near his own age, who had been brought up under very different circumstances. Two or three of these were inclined towards skepticism in religious things, and their reading was quite unlike that to which this boy had been accustomed. Some fascination of manner about them attracted the lad to their society, and he grew less and less fond of his truest and best friends. He became irregular in his attendance at the Sunday-school, and when remonstrated with by his teacher and friends had no candid and manly answer for them. After a while he ceased going to church entirely, spending his time at his lodgings reading profane and immoral books or in the society of his new companions. Then he found his way with these friends (so he called them, but they were really his greatest enemies) to taverns and even to worse places, reading a corrupt literature and thinking he was strengthening his mind and broadening his views. A little further on and his habits grew worse, and became the subject of observation and remark. His early friends interposed, talked kindly with him and received his promise to turn away from his evil associates (who had well-nigh ruined him) and to lead a better life. He promised well, and for a time things with him were better. But after a while he fell away again into his old ways and with his old tempters, and before his friends were aware of it he disappeared and went abroad. Then letters were received from him. He was without means; he found it hard to get employment; he had no references, and the people among whom he found himself were distrustful of strangers.

One of his friends to whom he wrote for a letter of recommendation replied something like this:

"It is impossible for me to give you a letter of recommendation except with qualification. If you are seeking employment it is your duty to make a candid statement of your condition. Make a clean breast of it. Keep nothing back. Say that you had a good situation; that you were growing with the growth of your employers; that your salary had been advanced twice within the year; that one of the partners was your friend; that he had stood by you in your earlier youth; that he had extricated you from embarrassment and would have helped you again when needed, and that in an evil hour you forgot this, and your duty to him and to the house which sustained you; that you left your place without your father's knowledge and well-nigh or quite broke his heart, and that all this grew out of your love of bad associates and your love of drink, and that while under this infatuation you went astray with bad women; and that in very despair of your ability to save yourself, and ashamed to meet your employers, you sought other scenes in the hope that in a new field and with new associates you could reform.

"If you say this or something like this to a Christian man, little as you affect to think of Christianity, his heart will open to you and you can then look him frankly in the face, and have no concealments from him. Any other course than this will only prolong your agony, and in the end plunge you in deeper shame and disgrace. If you will take this advice, you may yet make a man of yourself, and no one will be more rejoiced than myself or more ready to help you. Read the parable of the prodigal son every day; don't think so much of your fancied mental ability; get down off your stilts and be a man, a humble, penitent man, and make your father's last days cheerful, instead of blasting his life.

"You see that I am in earnest and that I feel a deep interest in you, else I would have thrown your letter to me into the fire."

I believe that this young man's fall was due entirely to the influence of his foolish, bad companions. And I know that this sad history is the record of many others; in fact, that the same experience awaits all who think it a light matter what company they keep, and who drift on the current with no purpose except to find pleasure, without regard to their duty to God. When I see, as I so often do, young men standing at the corners of the streets, or lounging against lamp-posts, and catch a word as I pass, very often profane or indecent, I know very well that a work of ruin is going on there, which, if unchecked, will certainly lead to destruction. And I wonder whether these boys and young men have parents or sisters, who love them and who yet allow them to pass unwarned down the road that leads to death.

But there are other companions, foolish, bad companions, besides those that appear to us in bodily form. They confront us in the printed page. You read a book or a pamphlet or paper which is full of dialogue. Such books are often more attractive than a plain narrative with little conversation. You enter fully, even if unconsciously, into the spirit of the story. The characters are real to you. You seem to see the forms before you; you make a picture of each in your mind, so that if you were an artist you could paint the portrait of each one. Sometimes the dialogue is full of profanity, and though you make no sound as you read, you are really pronouncing each word in your mind. And every time you say a bad word, in your mind, you defile your heart. You are in effect listening to bad words not spoken by other people merely, but spoken by yourself, and before you are aware of it you will be in the habit of thinking oaths when you are afraid to speak them out. It is even worse, if possible, when the language is obscene. Now do you ever think that when you are reading such wretched stuff you are in effect associating with the characters whose talk you are listening to, and without rebuke? They are thieves, pirates, burglars, dissolute, the very worst of society, even murderers. You may not have the courage to rebuke those who are defiling the very air with their foul talk; you may be too cowardly even to turn away from such company lest they sneer at you; but what do you say of a boy who deliberately, and after being warned, reads by stealth such stuff as I have described? Is there any one here who would be guilty of such conduct?

These evils of which I am speaking, and I do so most reluctantly, for these are not pleasant subjects — are not mere theories. They are sad realities. It was my ill fortune in my boyhood to know some boys who were essentially corrupt. Their minds were cages of unclean birds. They were inexpressibly vile. And it is this fear of the evil that one sinner may do among young boys that leads me to say what I do on this most painful subject. Oh, boys, if I can persuade you to turn away from foolish company, from bad associates, I shall feel that I am doing indeed a blessed work. For what is the object, the purpose of all this that is said to you? It is to make men of you and to give you grace and strength to assert your manhood. It is to build you up on the foundation of a substantial education, and so prepare you for the life that is before you here and for that life which is beyond. But the education of text-books illustrated by the best instructors is not enough; it is not all you need for the great work of your lives. You must be ready when you are equipped not only to take care of yourselves, but to help those who may be dependent upon you, for you are not to live for yourselves. And you cannot be fully equipped unless you have the blessing of Almighty God on your work and on your life.

I want you to be successful men, and no man can be a successful man, in the highest and best sense, unless he is a religious man. How can one expect to make his way in life as he ought, without the blessing of God? And how can one expect the blessing of God who does not ask God for his blessing? Prayers in the church are not enough; the reading of the Scriptures in the church is not enough; you must read the Scriptures for yourselves; you must pray for yourselves and each one for himself, as well as for others.

# ON THE DEATH OF PRESIDENT GARFIELD.

September 25, 1881.

I WISH to lead your thoughts to one of the strangest things—one of the most difficult things to understand, which has ever occurred. On the second day of July last the President of the United States, when about to step into a railway train which was to carry him North, where he was to attend a college commencement, at the college where he was graduated, was shot down by an assassin.

I say it is one of the strangest things, because the President did not know the assassin, and had never injured him nor any of his friends. There was absolutely no motive for the hideous deed.

I say it is most difficult to understand, because we believe that Divine Providence overrules all events, holds all power, and we wonder why He permitted the wretch to do so deplorable a deed.

President Garfield was no ordinary man. He was emphatically a man of the people. He was born in a log-cabin which his father had built with his own hands. It was a very small house, twenty feet by thirty. When James was two years old, his father

(69)

died, late in the autumn, and this boy with three other children were all dependent upon their mother for a support. How the lone widow passed that winter we do not know; but when the spring came there was a debt to be paid, and part of the farm had to go to pay it. About thirty acres of the clearing were left, and this little farm was worked by the mother and her oldest son. Only those who have lived on a farm in the country know how hard the work is. When James was five years old he was sent to school, a mile and a half away, and as this was a very long walk for so young a boy, his sister often carried the little boy on her back.

After a while the boy tried to learn the carpenter's trade, and in this effort he spent two years or so, going to school at intervals and studying at spare hours at home. So he mastered grammar, arithmetic and geography. After that he became a sort of general help and book-keeper for a manufacturer in the neighborhood at $14 per month "and found," and this was to him a very great advance. But not being well treated there, he soon left and took to chopping wood—at one time cutting about twenty-five cords for some $7. Then having read some tales of the sea, sailors' stories, such as you have often read, he wanted to be a sailor; but when he applied for a place on the great lake, he looked so like a landsman from the country that no captain would engage him. So he went to the canal, and found employment in leading or driving horses or mules on the tow-path. But he was soon promoted to be a deck-hand and steersman, and often falling into the water (once almost being drowned) and meeting some other mishaps, he concluded that "following the water" was not his forte, and he abandoned it. By this time he had saved some money, and his brother Thomas lent him some more, and with another young man and a cousin he went to a neighboring town to the academy. These young fellows rented a room, borrowed some simple cooking utensils, a table and some chairs, made beds and filled them with straw, and set up house-keeping, and went to the academy.

Young Garfield spent three years at this academy, doing odd jobs of carpenter work when he could, and so eking out a living. Then he went to an eclectic institute, and paid his way in part by doing the janitor's work of sweeping the floor and making the fires. Here he prepared himself to enter the junior class in a higher college, and, after some delay, he entered that class in Williams College, Massachusetts.

While pursuing his college course at Williams he filled his vacations by teaching in district schools in the neighborhood until his graduation, in 1856, at twenty-five years of age—quite advanced, you see, in years for a college graduate.

Then he went back as a teacher to his eclectic institute, became a professor of Greek and Latin, and then at twenty-eight years of age became a Senator in the Ohio Legislature. When the war broke out in 1861, while still a member of the State Senate, the Government commissioned him as colonel of a regiment, and he did good service in the State of Kentucky in driving out the rebels. In a few months he was promoted to be brigadier-general. So he went on distinguishing himself wherever he was placed, and, having been assigned for duty to the Army of the Cumberland, fighting his last battle at Chickamauga, his gallantry was so conspicuous and so successful that within a fortnight he was made a major-general.

While in the army he was elected representative to Congress, and on December 5, 1863, he took his seat in the House, the youngest member of Congress.

Some time after this, the war still going on, he wished to rejoin the army, but President Lincoln would not permit it, on the ground that his military knowledge would be invaluable to the government. After serving seventeen years in the House of Representatives, at times Chairman of most important committees, he was elected to the Senate, but before he took his seat he was nominated for the Presidency, and last November was elected by a large majority to that high office.

On the 4th of March last he was inaugurated, and

four months afterwards (July 2d) he fell by the hand of an assassin.

You know how during this long, dry, hot summer he has been lying in Washington until the last two weeks, hanging between life and death; and you know how tenderly and lovingly he has been nursed; how gently he was removed to the sea, in the hope that a change of air and scene would do what the best surgical and medical skill had failed to do; and you know how last Monday night, while you were sleeping soundly in your beds, the bells of our city and all over the land were tolling the tidings of his death.

He was a good man—in many respects as well qualified to fill the Presidential chair as any man who has ever sat in it. So I say it is most difficult to understand why he was taken away.

Like all of you he lost his father by death at an early age; as is the case with all of you his mother was poor. He struggled hard for an education, and he acquired it, who knows at what a cost! He was never satisfied with present attainments; he was always on the advance. At an early age he gave himself to the Lord, joining the church; and as that branch of the church does not believe in the necessity of ordination for the ministry he preached the Gospel as a layman, as the great Faraday preached in London and as Christian laymen preach the same truths to you, and it was my purpose, formed when he was elected in November last, to persuade him, some time when he might be passing through Philadelphia, to come to this chapel and address you boys. This, alas, now can never be.

President Garfield loved his mother. No more touching incident was ever witnessed than that which hundreds of people saw on inauguration day, when, after taking the oath of his high office, he turned immediately to his dear old mother and kissed her.

Our great sorrow is not felt by us alone. All nations mourn with us. The Queen of Great Britain with her own hand sends messages of the sweetest, the most touching sympathy. She, too, is a widow and her children are fatherless. She sends flowers for Mrs. Garfield and puts her court in mourning, a compliment never extended before except in the case of death in a royal family. Other European and Asiatic and African governments send their sympathy—they all feel it—they all deplore it. Emblems of mourning are displayed in every street in our city, and every heart is sad. The people mourn.

Boys, you may not be Presidents—probably not one here will ever be at the head of this nation; nor is this of any moment; but remember it was not only as President of the United States that General Garfield was wise and good—it was in every place where he was put; whether in school, in college, in teaching, in the army, in Congress, in the President's chair, in his family and on his sick and dying bed, languishing and suffering, wasting and burning with fever, exhausted by wounds cruel and undeserved, he was always the same brave, true, real man.

Some of you know with what profound and tender interest people gathered in places of prayer that Tuesday morning to ask that the journey from Washington to Long Branch might be safe and prosperous, and how the hope was expressed, almost to assurance, that the Saviour would meet his disciple by the sea. The prayer was granted. The Lord did meet his disciple, not, as was so much desired, with gifts of healing; nothing short of a miracle could do that, but by a more complete preparation of the people for the final issue. It came at last. And while many of us were sleeping quietly, telegraphic messages were flashing the sad intelligence everywhere that, at last, he was at rest.

Now that we know that he is taken away, we stand in awe and amazement. We cannot yet understand it.

Shall we gather a few lessons from his life? Some of the most apparent may be mentioned very briefly.

The simplicity of his character is most interesting. Conscious as he must have been of the possession of no ordinary mental force, he was never obtrusive nor self-assertive. What seemed to be his duty he did, with purpose and completeness. And his associates often placed him in positions of high trust and responsibility.

He was an accomplished scholar. Even while engrossed in Congressional duties, to a degree which left him little or no time for recreation, he did not fail to keep himself fresh in classic literature. It is said that a friend returning from Europe, and desiring to bring him some little present, could think of nothing more acceptable than a few volumes of the Latin poets.

When his life comes to be written by impartial hands, it will be found that along with his great simplicity and his high culture there will be most prominent his devotion to principle. This was his great characteristic. I have no time, and this is not the place, to speak of his adherence, under strong adverse influences, to his sound views on the great currency question which has occupied so much the attention of Congress.

In a not very remote sense his death is to be attributed to his devotion to principle. That great and most discreditable contest at Albany might have been settled weeks before it was, although in a very different manner, if the President could have yielded his convictions. He did not yield, and he was slain.

The funeral services in the capitol are over and the men whom Mrs. Garfield chose as the bearers of her husband's coffin were not members of the cabinet, nor senators, nor judges of the Supreme Court, any of whom would have been honored by such a service, but they were plain men, of names unknown to us, members of his own little church.

They are gone. They have taken his worn and wasted and mutilated form, all that remains in this world of the strong, pure life that was not yet fifty years old, to the beautiful city by the lake, and there within sight and almost within sound of the waves of the great inland sea, they will to-morrow lay him to rest until the morning of the resurrection.

.   .   .   .   .   .

What use shall we make of this deplorable calamity? Shall our faith in the prevalence of prayer be weakened? God forbid that we should so distort his teachings. "Nay, but, O man, who art thou that repliest against God?"

Our prayers are answered, not as we wished, and almost insisted, but in softening the hearts of the people and drawing them as they have never before been drawn towards the Great Ruler of the universe, and in uniting the people, and also in promoting a better feeling between the different sections of our country than has been known for half a century. And if, in addition to this, the people would only learn to abate that passion for office which has been so fatal to peace, and would be content to allow fitness for office to be the only rule of appointment, then a true civil service would be a heritage for the securing of which even the sacrifice of a President would seem not too great a price.

"And the archers shot at King Josiah, and the king said to his servants, Have me away for I am sore wounded. His servants therefore took him out of that chariot, and put him in the second chariot that he had, and they brought him to Jerusalem, and he died and was buried. And all Judah and Jerusalem mourned for Josiah." 2 Chron. xxxv. 23, 24.

# THE CASE OF THE UNEDUCATED EMPLOYED.

March 25, 1888.

A DISTINGUISHED lawyer of our city delivered an address before one of the societies in the venerable University of Harvard on this subject: "The Case of the Educated Unemployed." With an intimate knowledge of his subject, and with rare felicity of thought and expression, he set before his audience, most of whom were either in the learned professions or preparing to enter them, the overcrowded condition of those professions, especially that of the law, a preparation for which is supposed to imply a more or less thorough academic or collegiate education.

I have a different task; for I would show the importance of education to the workers with the hand, whether in the mills, the shops, or among the various trades and occupations. By education I do not mean that of the colleges, or of the common schools merely, but also that which is acquired sometimes without the advantage of any schools. And I particularly desire to show that an uneducated worker, whatever be his work, is at an immense disadvantage with one who is engaged in the same kind of work, and who is more or less educated.

A mechanic may be well trained; may have more than his share of brains; may be highly successful in his business; indeed, may have acquired a large property, and have very high credit, and may hardly know how to write his name. A man may have scores or hundreds of men in his employment, and be conducting business on a very large scale, indeed, and yet be so ignorant of accounts that he is entirely at the mercy of his book-keeper, and may be so defrauded as to be on the very brink of ruin and not know it until it is almost too late. In the course of a long business life more than one such case has come under my observation. A man may be partially educated, able to cast up accounts, able to keep books by double entry (and no other kind of book-keeping is worthy of the name), and yet not be able to write a simple agreement in good English, nor understand clearly the meaning of such a paper when written by another.

Very many of the business failures that occur are due to the fact that the person or firm did not know how to keep accounts. This is not confined to people of small business. How often after a failure are we told "that the man was very much surprised at his condition; he thought he was all right; he could not account for his failure, and that in a short time he would have his books in such a shape that he would be able to make a statement to his creditors and ask their advice. It would require ten days or so, however, before he could tell how he stood." Why, if the man had been an educated business man, and an honest man, he would have known in twenty-four hours how he stood.

The great majority of people who are employed are not educated. They do not know how to do in the best manner, that which they have to do. Perhaps a good definition of education, as the word is applied to a working man, may be that he knows how to do that which he has to do, in the very best way.

Education may be of three kinds, viz.:

That of the *schools*.

*Self-education*.

That of *trade* or *business*.

*That of the schools*. And this is the best of all; for the whole of one's time is given to it; and if you are so inclined you may go through the whole course, as provided in this school. And all this with text-books, instruments and other appliances, absolutely free of cost. A boy, therefore, who passes through the entire course of study here, has superior opportunities of acquiring a most substantial education.

Certainly the education of the schools is the best; and let me urge you with all seriousness to make the best use of your opportunities. You can never learn as easily as now. You are young. You are not burdened with cares. Do not relax your efforts in the least; do not yield to weariness; do not think you know enough already; do not be impatient lest others of your own age, who have already left school to go to work, get ahead of you in trade or in any kind of business; if they have the start of you, they may not be able to keep it; and depend upon it, in the long run you will overtake and pass them, other things being equal, if you have a better school education than they have. When you are told that young men who are well educated are thereby unfitted or unwilling to take the lowest places in trade or business, do not believe it. I know the contrary. The better the school education you have, and the more you know, the more valuable you will be to your employer.

Another kind of education is called, but most inaccurately, *self-education*. All that I mean by it is, that education which one acquires without teachers. As so defined, it may be divided into two parts, viz.: the incidental and the direct.

Let me speak first of the *incidental*.

I mean by this that education that comes to us from society.

You cannot live alone, and you ought not to if you could. You seek companions, or other persons will seek you. Let your associates be those whose friendship will be an instruction to you, rather than simply a means of social enjoyment. There are young

THE CASE OF THE UNEDUCATED EMPLOYED. 83

people of both sexes who, without being vicious, are utterly weak and foolish, idle and listless, drifting along a current, the end of which they do not care to think of. They are living for this life only, with no thought of the future, no ambition, mere butterflies, who float in the sunshine when the sun is shining, but who, in a dark and cloudy day, are bored and miserable, and utterly useless. Sometimes they are pleasant enough to chat with for a few minutes, but to be shut up to such companionship as this, would be intolerable. Society has a large element of this description, and you are likely to see it in your daily life.

But this is not the worst phase of life among the young people with whom you may be thrown. There are worse elements than this. There are those who are depraved to a degree quite beyond their age; who have given themselves up to work all uncleanness with greediness; who put no restraint on their inclinations; in whose eyes nothing is pure or sacred; who have no respect for that which is wholesome or decent; who are the devil's own children, and who are not ashamed of their parentage. And to such baleful, deadly influences and associations will you be exposed, my young friends, and you may not be apprised of their true character until it is too late.

But there are *direct* means of education, so called.

The first of these which I mention is the use of books. This is unquestionably the best means. I am supposing that you have some taste for reading; if you have not, it is hardly worth while for me to speak, or for you to listen. I know some people who rarely read a book, and I pity them. They seem to think that all that is necessary to read is the daily newspaper. I do not say that such persons are necessarily very ignorant, for very much may be learned from the daily paper. But the newspaper does not pretend to supply all that you need, to fit you for a life of business, either as a dealer in merchandise, a professional man or a mechanic. No; you must read books, not only for entertainment and recreation, but for information and culture, which you can obtain nowhere else. If there is no public library within your reach, seek out some kind-hearted man or woman who has books, and who will be willing to lend them to one who is in search of knowledge. I well remember a gentleman in my early life who did this kind office for me before I was able to buy books, and there are such now who will do the same for you.

If you have little knowledge of books, you ought to ask the advice of some practical friend to point out such as you may most safely and properly read. For if left to your own judgment or taste, you will probably waste valuable time, or be discouraged by an attempt to read something not immediately necessary or appropriate. But do not attempt to follow an elaborate plan of reading, such as you will find detailed in some books, for you are very likely to be discouraged by the greatness of the task. Such lists, I fancy, are made out by scholars who have read almost everything, and to whom reading is no task whatever, and who have plenty of time. Do not attempt to read too many books, nor too much at a time, and do not be disappointed or discouraged if you are not able to remember or put to good account all that you read. You cannot always know what particular kind of food has afforded you the most nourishment. You may rest assured, however, that as every morsel of food that you take and are able to digest does something to build up and develop your system, or repair its waste, so every book or paper that you read, that is wholesome, does something, you may not know how much, to strengthen or develop your mind.

There are books that you read for entertainment or recreation, and that are written for that purpose only. You may read such; indeed, you ought to read them, for you need, as everybody else needs, recreation and amusement, and there is much of the purest and best of this that you can get from books. But you must not make the mistake of supposing that most, or even a very large proportion, of your reading can be of this character. You would not think of making your daily meals of the articles of food that you enjoy as the sweets of your meals. You would not think of living on sponge-cake and ice-cream for a regular diet. You might as well do so, as to read only the light and humorous matter that was never intended for the mental diet of a working man. No. If you would attain the real object of reading and study, you must read and study books and papers that tax the full powers of your mind to understand them. This will soon strengthen the quality of your mind, even as the exercise of your muscles in work or play will develop a strength of body that the idle or lazy youth knows nothing of.

If you would know how to make yourself master of any book that you read, form the habit, if the book is your own, of making notes with a pencil in the margin of the pages; but if the book is not your property, or in any case, take a sheet of paper and write at the end of every chapter questions on the matter discussed, and the answer to such questions will probably bring out the author's meaning so fully that you will have *absorbed* the book and made it your own; for, as an eminent American author has said, " thought is the property of whoever can entertain it."

I said just now that the daily newspaper does not pretend to supply all that you need to fit you for a life of business, either as a dealer in goods, or as a mechanic or clerk. But the daily paper is a most important means of education—so important that no one can afford to ignore it. Now-a-days one cannot be well informed who does not read the newspaper.

## THE CASE OF THE UNEDUCATED EMPLOYED. 87

The whole world is brought before us every morning and evening, and, if we do not read the news as it comes, we shall not know what we ought to know. It is not necessary to read everything in a daily paper; there are some things that it will be better for you not to read. You need not read all the editorials, brilliant as some of them are, for sometimes they discuss subjects that are not at all interesting nor useful to you. The newspaper from which I make the most clippings is one which is the fullest of advertisements, but which sometimes has nothing whatever in it that I read. But when it does discuss a subject of interest, it is apt to leave nothing further to be said.

But to read with the most advantage one ought to have within easy reach a dictionary, an atlas and, if possible, an encyclopedia. Then you can read with profit, and the mere outlines which the newspaper gives can be filled up by reference to books which give more or less complete histories.

The political articles which appear in the height of a campaign are hardly worth reading, unless you think of entering politics as a money-making business, which I sincerely hope none of you think of doing. And I am sure that the full accounts of crime, and especially the details of police reports and criminal trials, you will do well to pass by and not read. I really believe that a familiarity with these details prepares the way, in many instances, for the commission of crime, just as the reading of accounts of suicide sometimes leads to the act itself.

Some of the best minds in our country, and in the world, are now employed in writing for the periodicals and magazines. No one can be well informed without reading something of the vast amount of matter which is thus poured out before him. I have not named the newspapers nor the magazines which you may read with the most profit; but your teachers can advise you what to read. Rather is it important for you to know what *not* to read. Many of the most popular and the most useful books that have been published within the last quarter of a century have appeared first in the pages of a weekly or monthly paper. The best thoughts of the best thinkers sometimes first see the light in such pages.

Besides the newspaper and the literary magazine, there are scientific periodicals, which are of essential value to a worker who wishes to be well informed in any of the mechanical arts. The *Scientific American* is, perhaps, the best of this class, both in the beauty of its illustrations and in the high quality of its contributions. The *Popular Science Monthly* is a periodical of a wider range and more diversified character. These periodicals, if you are not able to subscribe for them as individuals or in clubs, you may find in the public library. But let me urge you to turn away from "dime novels." Not because they are cheap, but because they are often unwholesome and immoral. The vile, fiery, poisonous whiskey which so many wretched creatures drink until the coatings of the stomach are destroyed, and the brain is on fire, is no more fatal to the health and life, than is the immoral literature I speak of, to the mind and soul of him who reads. There is an abundance of good literature that is cheap—do not read the bad.

Having now spoken of the education you may get in the schools, and that which you may acquire for yourselves, if you have the pluck to strive for it, either in the society which you cultivate, or more directly from books, whether read as an entertainment and recreation, or, better still, by careful study; or through the daily newspaper, or the periodical, whether literary or scientific; or, what is best of all, that which is decidedly religious; I turn now to the education which you will acquire when you work day by day at your trade or business.

Let me beg of you to consider the great value of truthfulness in all your training. Hardly anything will help you more to reach up towards the top. And when you are at the head of an establishment of your own or somebody else's (and I take it for granted you will be at the head some day), whether it be a workshop or factory of any kind, or a store, no matter what, a fixed habit of keeping your word, of not promising unless you are certain of keeping your promise, will almost insure your success if you are a good workman. How many good mechanics have utterly failed of success because they have not cared to keep their promises? A firm of high reputation agrees to supply certain articles of furniture at a time fixed by them. The time comes but the articles do not come. A call of inquiry is made and new promises are made only to be broken. Excuses are offered and more promises given; then incomplete articles are sent; then more delays, until, when patience is nearly exhausted, the work is finished. Then comes the bill and there is a mistake in it. The whole transaction is a series of disappointments and misunderstandings. Will you ever incline to go to that place again?

It is usual for miners of coal to place their sons, as they become ten or twelve years of age, at the foot of the great breakers to watch the coal as it comes rattling and broken down the great wire screens, and catch the pieces of slate and throw them to one side and allow only the pure coal to pass down into the huge bins, from which it is dropped into the cars and taken to market. To an uneducated eye there is hardly any perceptible difference between the coal and the slate. But these little fellows soon become so quick in the education of the eye, that they can tell in an instant the difference. When the boy grows older he graduates to the place of a mule driver, and has his car and mule, which he drives day by day from the mouth of the mine to the breaker. Then when he begins to be of age he fixes his little oil lamp in the front of his cap, and goes down into the mines with his pick and becomes a miner of coal. It seems a dreary life to spend most of one's time under the ground, shut out from the sunshine and from the pure air. And most of these men having no education, and never having been urged to seek one, are content to spend all their days in this manner. But occasionally there is one who feels that he is capable of better things than this. And I know one at least, who began his work at the foot of a coal breaker and worked his way up through all these stages, as I have told you, and who determined to do something better for himself. So he gave much of his leisure (and everybody has some leisure) to study; nor was he discouraged by the difficulties in his way. He persevered. He rose to be a boss among the men; then having saved some money, instead of wasting it at the tavern, he bought his teams, and then bought an interest in a coal mine, and became a miner of his own coal, and had his men under him, and has grown to be a rich man, and is not ashamed of his small beginnings nor of his hard work. This is only one instance of success in rising from a low position to a high one.

The same thing is going on all around us and we see it every day. It would hardly be proper to give you names, but I could tell you of many within my own knowledge who, from positions of extremely hard labor and plain living, have risen to be the head men in shops and other places which they entered at the lowest places. Such changes are continually occurring. And there is no reason whatever, except your indifference, to prevent many of you from becoming, if God gives you health, the head men, in the places where you begin work as subordinates or in very low positions. And I tell you what you know already, that there is plenty of room for advancement. It is the lowest places that are full to overflowing. Who ever heard of a strike among the *chiefs* of any industry? No, indeed. They have made themselves indispensable to their employers and they don't need to strike. And there is hardly a youth who cannot by strict attention to business, and conscientious devotion to the interests of his employer, make himself so invaluable that he need not join any trades union for protection. Do the vast army of clerks in the various corporations, or in the great commercial houses, or in the public service, or in the army and navy—do these people ever band themselves in any associations like the trades unions? They know better than that; they accomplish their purposes in better ways. If the working classes, so called, were better educated, they would not suffer themselves to be led by the nose by people who will not themselves work, who will not touch even with their little fingers the burdens which are crushing the life out of the deluded ones whom they are leading to folly. It is a true education that is needed, a

## THE CASE OF THE UNEDUCATED EMPLOYED. 93

true conscience that must be cultivated, to enable men to do their own thinking, and to determine for themselves what are their best interests.

I urge you all to seek that higher and better education which will make you true men. You have now the great advantage of the education of the school. I have tried very simply, but not the less earnestly, to show you how you can fit yourselves for high places. It is for you to say whether you will avail yourselves of these plain hints. No earthly power can force you to do that which you will not do. You may lead a horse to a brimming fountain of water, but if he is not thirsty, no coaxing nor threatening nor beating can make him drink. I may show you, to demonstration, the abundant fountain of learning, but I can't make you drink, or even stoop to taste the stream, if you are not thirsty. I can't make you study, however great the advantage to you, or however much they who are interested in you desire that you should.

Every year this question which I have been pressing upon you becomes more and more important. The great colleges of the country are graduating their thousands of students, many of whom will compete with you for the high places in the mechanic arts. So are the public schools of the country sending out hundreds of thousands, many of them having the same aim. Technical schools, teaching the mechanic arts, are multiplying. Great changes have been made recently in our own city in this respect. The Spring Garden Institute is doing a noble work in this way. Our own college is moving in the same direction, and soon it will be sending out its hundreds every year to compete for places in the shops, with this great advantage, that you Girard boys have a school education—the best that you are able to receive, and you must not let any others go ahead of you.

Look at the poor, ignorant people from abroad who sweep our streets—look at the stevedores who load and unload the ships—look at the men who carry the hod of mortar or bricks up the high and steep ladders—look at the drivers and the conductors on our street cars, the most hard worked people among us—and are you not sure that most of these people are *un*educated? No one wants to be at the bottom all the time. We may have been there at the first; but those who have made the most progress are generally those who have had the best education. I know that education is not a sure guarantee of success; many other things enter into the consideration of the question; but I am saying that, other things being equal, *he who knows the most will do the best.* There are, alas, many instances of the sons of the rich, who have been well educated, who have everything provided for them, who have no stimulus, no spur; who have no regular occupation, and need not have any; many of whom sink into idleness and dis-

## THE CASE OF THE UNEDUCATED EMPLOYED. 95

sipation, and their fine education goes for nothing. But you are not of this class. You will have to make your way in the world by your own exertions.

I shall fail of my duty if I do not say some words about such boys as sometimes stand at the corners of the streets in large or small companies and amuse themselves by smoking and chewing tobacco, telling bad stories and making remarks upon those who pass by. I am sure much of this arises from thoughtlessness; but I wish to point out the exceeding impropriety of this behavior. I have known ladies to cross the street and, at much inconvenience, go quite out of their way rather than pass within hearing of these boys and young men. What right has any one to make the streets disagreeable to any passenger, to block up the way or make loose or rude remarks, or defile the pavement over which I walk?

All this most serious waste of time is probably because no one has particularly called attention to it. The time may come when you will recall the words of advice which you hear to-day, and you may regret when it is too late that you turned a deaf ear to what was said.

I have now tried, in as much detail as the time will permit, to show the importance of that education which will enable you to rise in your trade or business, whatever it may be, to the upper places; and I have tried to show that a true ambition leads one to strive to be *chief* rather than a *subordinate*, to be a *foreman* rather than a *journeyman*.

But, after all, everything will depend upon yourselves and upon God. There is no royal road to education; the very meaning of the word shows this; the mind must be drawn out, worked over, developed, rounded, hammered, somewhat as a blacksmith puts a piece of rough iron in the coals, keeps it there until it is red-hot, then draws it out, lays it upon his anvil and hammers it, turning it over and over, striking it first on this side and then on that, rounding it off; then when it cools thrusting it among the coals again, then hammering away again until he has brought the rough piece of iron to the size and shape he wishes, when he allows it to cool and harden. If you are willing to work your mind into the shape you want it, you will surely bring yourself to the front among active, ingenious and successful men. But this means hard work, and work all the time.

Now if you mean to avail yourselves of any of the hints which I have given you, if you really mean to succeed, if you are not content to be workers low down in the scale of industry, if you mean to rise rather than to be obscure, if you intend to be well-to-do men, instead of living from hand to mouth, you must grapple with the subject with all your might and keep at it all the time. And you must keep out of the streets at night, away from the taverns and from the low theatres, and from gambling dens, and from other places which I will not name; and, in short, you must be true Americans, for there is no truer type of manhood in all the world than a real American; and nowhere else in all the world has a poor boy so good an opportunity to be and do all this, as in our own good city of Philadelphia.

# WILLIAM PENN.

### October 22, 1882.

In the early autumn of the year 1682, a vessel with her bow pointing towards the west was making her way slowly across the Atlantic ocean. She was a small craft, rigged as a ship, and crowded with emigrants. The discomforts of a long and tiresome voyage, the very small accommodations, the horror of sea-sickness, were in this vessel aggravated by the breaking out of that most awful of all scourges, the small-pox. In a very short time, out of a population of one hundred, thirty passengers died. No record is left of the incidents of that voyage except this; but it is easy to imagine that all the circumstances were as deplorable as they could well be.

After a weary time of head winds and calms, in about seven weeks, this ship, the "Welcome," came within the capes of the Delaware bay.

The most distinguished person on that little ship was William Penn. He had left his home in England, embarking with his trusty friends in a vessel only one-tenth the size of the ships of our American

Line, to come to Pennsylvania. He had bought the whole province from the government of England for the sum of £16,000 sterling, which, measured by our money, is about $80,000, and this money was due to him for services rendered and money loaned to the government by his father, an admiral in the English navy.

About the 24th of October the vessel reached the town of Newcastle, where Penn landed and was cordially received by the people of that little village. Afterwards they came farther up the river to Uplands, now the town or city of Chester. Then, leaving the vessel here, they came in a barge (Penn and some of his principal men) to the mouth of Dock creek, the foot of what is now known as Dock street, where they landed, near a little tavern called the Blue Anchor.

There was already a settlement on the shore of the Delaware river, and the people, mostly Swedes, had built a little church somewhat farther down the stream. The entire land between the Delaware and Schuylkill rivers, and for a mile north and south, was owned by three brothers, Swedes, named Swen. Penn bought this tract from them, and at once proceeded to lay out his new city. When he bought the whole province from the crown he desired to call it New-Wales, because it was so hilly, but the king insisted on calling it Penn's Sylvania, in memory of the admiral, William's father. But when the new city came to be named, Penn having no one to dispute his wish, called it by that word, of whose meaning we think so little, Philadelphia—brotherly love. Two months after this he met the Indians, it is said, under a great elm tree in the upper part of the city, in what we now call Kensington, and concluded that treaty which has been said to be the only treaty that was ever made without an oath, and that was never broken. Shortly after this Penn proceeded to lay out the city, and, as a distinguished English author has said, he must have taken the ancient Babylon for his model, for this was the first modern city that was laid out with the streets crossing each other at right angles.

The charter which Penn received from Charles the Second, King of England (the original of which is in the capital at Harrisburg, on three large sheets of parchment), makes him proprietary and governor, also holding his authority under the crown. He at once therefore set about making a code of laws as special statutes, which with the common law of England should be the laws of the province. One of these special laws was this: "Every one, rich or poor, was to learn a useful trade or occupation; the poor to live on it: the rich to resort to it if they should become poor." And I do not know what better law he could have enacted.

When the news of Penn's arrival and cordial reception reached England and the continent of Europe, the effect was to arouse a spirit of emigration. Although Penn's first thought and purpose was to found a colony, where he and others who held the religious views of the Society of Friends might worship without hindrance (which liberty was denied them in England), the people from other countries in Europe came here in great numbers for other purposes. The population therefore multiplied rapidly, and the people were generally such as had determined to brave the privations of a new country, to make themselves a home where life could be lived under better conditions than in the old countries, under the harsh government of tyrannical kings. This emigration was stimulated also by the very liberal terms which the governor offered to new-comers; for to actual settlers he offered the land at about ten dollars for a hundred acres, subject, however, to a quit-rent of a quarter of a dollar an acre per annum forever; and this may be the origin of that ground-rent instrument which is almost peculiar to Pennsylvania, and which is such a favorite investment for our rich men.

After a stay of two years Penn returned to England, where he had left his wife and children; the care of the government having been left with a council, of which Thomas Lloyd was president, who kept the great seal.

Not long after his return to England the king, Charles the Second, died, and having no son he was succeeded by his brother, James Duke of York, as James the Second. Although Penn was on the most cordial terms with the new king, as he had been with Charles, this did not secure him from the repeated annoyances and persecutions of those who detested his religion. So severe was the treatment to which he was subjected, and such was his personal danger from unprincipled men, that he escaped to France. But not being able nor willing to bear this exile, he returned to England, was tried for his offence against the law of the church and was acquitted. After this he came to America again, intending to spend the rest of his life here, but he remained only two years.

The rest of his life was spent in England, but it was a life broken by persecutions and trials at law and other annoyances, the expenses of which, added to the losses by the unfaithfulness of his stewards, were so great as seriously to involve him in financial embarrassments; and he was even compelled to mortgage his great estate in Pennsylvania to relieve himself; but the interest annually payable on such encumbrance was so heavy that he felt the necessity of relieving himself of the property entirely, and he offered to sell it to the crown. While the matter was under consideration, his health began to decline; however, the terms were agreed upon, but while the papers were in the course of preparation he died peacefully at Rushcombe, in Buckinghamshire, July

30, 1718, and was buried five days after in the **burial** ground belonging to Jordan's meeting house.

Such is the briefest outline of the life of the founder of this commonwealth of Pennsylvania, and of this city of Philadelphia.

Let us see now what there was in this life which we may find it interesting to recall and dwell upon; what there was in it which may be useful for us to consider in its application to ourselves.

William Penn was born in the city of London on the 14th of October, 1644, in the parish of St. Catharine's, near the Tower. His father was an admiral and his grandfather was a captain in the English navy. Then, as now, it was the custom of English families of good condition to send their boys away from home to school. This boy, an only son, was therefore sent to school near the town of Wanstead, in Essex, called Chigwell. Here he remained until he was thirteen years old, with no incident particularly worthy of notice, except that he was, at the age of twelve, brought under deep religious impressions, which, however, like many other boys, he soon threw aside. He seems to have been apt to learn, and was fond of the childish sports belonging to his age. For two years after leaving school, he was under private instruction at home, until he was fifteen years old, when he entered the University of Oxford. Here he devoted himself most diligently to his studies and became a successful student. But this did not prevent him from entering most heartily into the sports which were common to young men of his quality. He was very fond of boating, fishing, shooting, and other pleasures, and he was extremely handsome; but he avoided dissipation of all kinds, thus proving that the keenest enjoyment of healthful sports is quite consistent with a pure life. If the college students of this day would believe and act upon this principle, it would be better for them and better for the world.

With this hearty enjoyment of sports, and this diligent application to study, he had a very tender sympathy and love for domestic animals. Towards those that were the most helpless, he evinced a kindliness that was almost womanly.

But he had a strong will, and it was impossible to turn him aside from a course of duty, when he was satisfied that it was real duty. During his school and college life there were many seasons of religious interest in his experience, and he was at last brought (under the preaching of a member of the Society of Friends named Thomas Loe) to declare himself a member of that society. He therefore refused to attend the services of the Church of England. The custom of wearing surplices by Oxford students, which had been abolished in Cromwell's time, had been restored by Charles; but Penn, when he came out as a religious man, threw off his surplice and refused to wear it. This act was bad enough in the eyes of the authorities; but his zeal went further than this, and, in common with some others of the same way of thinking, he so far forgot himself as to attack other students and tear off their surplices. This very grave offence could not be overlooked, and, admiral's son though he was, he was expelled from the University of Oxford. This was a great blow to his father, who was building the fondest hopes on the advancement of his son at college and his career as a courtier. No persuasion, however, could induce the son to reconsider his conduct, and his father at last flogged him and drove him from the house. Some time after this, through the intercession of the mother, the young man was brought back to his home; and his father, in the hope that a change of scene and circumstances would work a change in the lad's feelings, sent him to Paris, and to travel on the continent.

While in Paris he studied the French language, and read some books in theology, and went as far as Turin, in Italy, from whence, however, he was recalled to take charge of a part of his father's affairs. He then studied law for a year, which no doubt was of some help to him in the founding of his commonwealth. Then his father sent him to take care of his estates in Ireland, at that time under the viceroyalty of the Duke of Ormond. He entered the army here, and did good service too; and was, apparently, so much pleased with his new life that he suffered the only portrait of him that was ever painted, to be taken when he was wearing armor and in uniform. This picture, or a copy of it, may now be seen at the Historical Society of Pennsylvania, in Spruce street, above Eighth.

About this time he came again under the influence of the preacher Loe, and was recalled by his father, who remonstrated with him on his new mode of life, but with no success whatever. He would not give up his new religion. His father tried to compromise the matter with him, and he even went so far as to propose to his son, that if he would remove his hat in the presence of the king and the Duke of York and his father, as his superiors, their differences might be healed; but the son, believing that the removal of his hat would be dishonorable to God, absolutely refused.

His life for some time after this was stormy enough. He came out boldly and in defiance of law as a preacher of the Society of Friends; and was repeatedly imprisoned, sometimes in the Tower of London and sometimes in the loathsome prison of Newgate, from which places he was released by the intercession of the Duke of York and his father and other friends.

Those were very rough times, not likely, let us hope, to be repeated. Society was very corrupt at the highest sources, and religion was more violent and aggressive in its measures then than now. The world has grown wiser and better—there is more toleration, more of the Spirit of the Master now than then, and in our favored land every soul can worship God as he may choose to do.

William Penn was a *statesman*. He founded this great commonwealth of Pennsylvania. He established a code of laws that were in advance of his time. He stipulated that the law of primogeniture, that law which gives the lands of the father to the *oldest* son, with little or no provision for younger sons, that law which is the corner-stone of the crown of England, should have no place in this new commonwealth. The property of a parent dying without a will should be *equally divided among his children*. Penn was a statesman in the broadest sense of the term. His laws were for the greatest good of the greatest number. He treated the Indians as if they were human beings, and not as if they were brute beasts. Indeed, he never treated the brutes as the Indians have been treated even in our day by harsh and unscrupulous agents of the government. Whether he was exactly just in his dealings with Lord Baltimore, the settler of Maryland, I do not know. Perhaps he was not. We know this misunderstanding gave him great trouble, and was indeed the prime cause of his return to England.

Penn was a *rich man*. The inheritance left him by his father was handsome, and he could have lived most comfortably upon it. But when he received from the crown the charter which made him the owner of Pennsylvania, he was the largest landholder, except sovereigns, known in history. He did not use his wealth for personal indulgence, or for luxurious living for himself or his family. He believed that he held his property as a trustee, and that he had no right to waste it. He might have lived the life of an ordinary English nobleman (for it is said his father was offered a peerage), but such a life had no charms for him.

Penn was a *conscientious man*. I mean by this that he followed his inner convictions, without regard to consequences. What he wanted to know was, whether a given thing was *right* and according to his way of determining what the right was; and he did it if it were a duty, without flinching. No personal inconvenience, no consideration for the views or wishes of other people, was allowed to stand in the way of his duty, as he understood it. It was the custom of that time for gentlemen to wear swords, as some gentlemen now carry canes, and with no purpose except as an ornament or part of the dress. Some time after he joined the Society of Friends, and while still wearing his sword, he said to his friend George Fox, "Is it consistent with our principles and our testimonies against war for me to wear my sword?" When Fox replied, "Wear thy sword as usual, so long as thy conscience will permit it." This friendly rebuke led him to lay aside his sword never to resume it.

William Penn was a *religious man*. He was called by the Holy Spirit at the early age of twelve years, as I have already said. He resisted that call and many others, until under faithful preaching he could resist no longer, when he yielded himself to the divine call and became an open professor of the principles of the Society of Friends. This was a very different thing, so far as personal comfort was concerned, from professing religion in the ordinary forms; for this was to join a hated sect, and bear all the contempt and persecution that belonged to a profession of religion in the early days of Christianity, when men, women and children perilled their lives in the service of the great Master. But Penn cared not for the cost; he was ready to go to prison, and to death if necessary, for his opinions. He *did* go to prison over and over again, and bore right manfully all that was put upon him. He was not idle, however, in the prison. He preached to his fellow-prisoners; he wrote pamphlets; he did everything in his power to make known to others the good tidings of salvation that had come to him. He wrote a great many letters, and they were all full of the spirit of religion. He wrote treatises on religious truth, that might have been written by a systematic theologian; but among the most practical things he wrote was the address to his children, that it would be well if all people would read, and which, with a few exceptions, is as appropriate for the people of to-day as it was for those who lived two hundred years ago.

If Penn had not been a religious man, his life had not been worth recording. He would have lived the life that was lived by almost all men of his class at that time, a life of unrestrained worldliness and luxury. The Almighty, who had great purposes in store for the New World, to be wrought out by the instrumentality of man, could have chosen another man, but he chose Penn.

Such is the story of the life of a man who was one of the world's heroes. His name will never die. There is a large literature on the subject of his life, some of which you will find in your own library, if you choose to look further into it. This is all that I feel it proper to say to you to-day about it.

Boys, it is a great thing to have been born in Pennsylvania, as all of you were. And this could hardly be said of any other congregation in this city to-day. This is a great commonwealth. As to its size, it is (leaving out Wales) nearly as large as the whole of England. As to great rivers and mountains and mines and metals, as to forests and fields, we are far in advance of anything of the kind in England. No valleys on earth are more beautiful or more productive than the valleys of our own Pennsylvania.

It is a great thing, boys, to have been born in the city of Philadelphia, as most of you were. It was founded by a great and good man. There are, in the civilized world, but three cities that are larger than ours. There is no city, except London, that has so many dwelling-houses, and there is none anywhere in all the world where the poor man who works for his living can live so happily and so well.

In this State, in this city, your lot is cast. You will soon many of you take your place among the citizens, and have your share in choosing the men who make and execute the laws. Some of you *will be* the men who make and execute the laws. William Penn founded this commonwealth, not only to provide a peaceable home for the persecuted members of his own society, but to afford an asylum for the good and oppressed of every nation; and he founded an empire where the pure and peaceable principles of Christianity might be carried out in practice. When you come to take your part in the duties of public life, see to it that you forget not his wise and noble purpose.

# OUR CONSTITUTION.

October, 1887.

I AM about to do what I have never done—what has probably never been done by any other person in this chapel. I propose to give you a political speech, but not a partisan speech; indeed, I hardly think you will be able to guess, from anything I say, to which of the two great political parties I belong.

I do not go to the Bible for a text—though there are many passages in the holy Scriptures which would answer my purpose very well—but I take for my text the following passage from the will of Mr. Girard:

"AND ESPECIALLY I DESIRE THAT BY EVERY PROPER MEANS, A PURE ATTACHMENT TO OUR REPUBLICAN INSTITUTIONS, AND TO THE SACRED RIGHTS OF CONSCIENCE AS GUARANTEED BY OUR HAPPY CONSTITUTIONS, SHALL BE FORMED AND FOSTERED IN THE MINDS OF THE SCHOLARS."

A few weeks ago our city was filled to overflowing with strangers. They came from all parts of the land, and some from distant parts of the world. Our railways and steamboats were crowded to their utmost capacity. Our streets were thronged; our hotels and many private dwellings were full. It was said that there were half a million of strangers here. The President of the United States, the members of the Cabinet, many members of the national Senate and House of Representatives, the general of the army and many other generals, the highest navy officers, judges of the Supreme Court of the United States and of the State courts, the governors of most of the States—each with his staff—soldiers and sailors of the United States, and many regiments of State troops (the Girard College cadets among them)—a military and naval display of twenty-five thousand men—representatives of foreign states, an exhibition of the industrial and mechanic arts, in a procession miles in extent, such as was never seen in all the world before; receptions and banquets, public and private; a general suspension of most kinds of business—all this occurred in the streets of our city, only a few weeks ago. What did it mean?

It was the One Hundredth Anniversary of the adoption of the Constitution of the United States, and it was considered to be an event of such importance that it was well worth while to pause in our daily work; to give holiday to our schools; to still the busy hum of industry; to stop the wheels of commerce; to close our places of business.

One hundred years ago the Constitution of the United States of America was adopted in this city.

What had been our government before this time? Up to July, 1776, there had been thirteen colonies, all under the government of Great Britain. In the lapse of time, the people of these colonies, owing allegiance to the king of England, and subjected to certain taxes which they had no voice in considering and imposing, because they had no representation in the Parliament which laid the taxes, became discontented and rebellious, and in a convention which sat in our own city of Philadelphia, on the 4th of July, 1776, they united in a DECLARATION OF INDEPENDENCE of Great Britain, and announced the thirteen colonies as Free, Sovereign and Independent States.

This, however, was only a DECLARATION; and it took seven long years of exhausting and terrible war (which would have been longer still but for the timely aid of the French nation) to secure that independence and have it acknowledged by the governments of Europe.

Before the DECLARATION, each of the colonies had a State government and a written constitution for the regulation of its internal affairs. Now these colonies had become States, with the necessity upon them (not at first admitted by all) of a general compact or agreement, by which the States, while maintaining their independence in many things, should become a confederated or general government.

More than a year passed before the Constitution, which the Convention agreed upon, was adopted by a sufficient number of the States to make it binding on all the thirteen; and I am glad to know and to say that my own little State of Delaware was the first to adopt it.

Now, WHAT IS THE CONSTITUTION? How does it differ from the *laws* which the Congress enacts every winter in Washington?

First, let me speak of other nations. There are two kinds of government in the world—monarchical and republican. And there are two kinds of monarchies—absolute and limited. An absolute monarch, whether he be called emperor or king, rules by his personal will—HIS WILL IS THE LAW. One of the most perfect illustrations of absolute or personal government is seen on board any ship, where the will of the chief officer, whether admiral or captain, or whatever his rank, is, and must be, the law. From his orders, his decisions, there is no appeal until the ship reaches the shore, when he himself comes under the law. This is a very ancient form of government, now known in very few countries calling themselves civilized.

The other kind of monarchy is limited by a constitution, *un*written, as in Great Britain, or *written*, as in some other nations of Europe. In these countries the sovereigns are under a constitution; in some instances with hardly as much power as our President. They are not a law unto themselves, but are under the common law.

The other kind of government is republican, democratic or representative. It is, as was happily said on the field of Gettysburg, long after the battle, by President Lincoln, " a government *of* the people, *by* the people, *for* the people." These few plain words are well worth remembering—" of," " by," " for " the people. These are the traits which distinguish our government from all kinds of monarchies, whether absolute or limited, hereditary or elective.

After the war between Germany and France, in 1870, the German kingdoms of Prussia, Hanover, Saxony, Wurtemberg, Bavaria, with certain small principalities, each with its hereditary sovereign, were consolidated or confederated as the German empire, and the king of Prussia, the present Frederick William, was crowned emperor of Germany.

France, however, after that war, having had enough of kings and emperors, adopted the republican form of government. So that now there are three republics in Europe, viz.: France, Switzerland, and a little territory on the east coast of Italy, San Marino.

So that almost all of Europe, all of Asia, and all of Africa (except Liberia), and the islands of Australia, and the northern part of North America (except Alaska), are under the government of monarchs; while the three countries of Europe already mentioned, and our own country, and Mexico, and the Central American States, and all South America except Brazil (and some small parts of the coast of South America under British rule), are republics.*

Now let us come back to our own government and see what is, and whether it is better than any form of monarchy; and if so, why.

What is the CONSTITUTION OF THE UNITED STATES? The first clause in it is the best answer I can give:

"WE, THE PEOPLE OF THE UNITED STATES, in order to form a more perfect union, establish justice, insure domestic tranquillity, provide for the common defence, promote the general welfare, and secure the blessings of liberty to ourselves and our posterity, do ordain and establish this Constitution for the United States of America."

Then follow the articles and sections setting forth the principles on which it was proposed to build up a nation in this western world. The thirteen States each had its constitution and its laws, but *this instrument* was intended to serve as the foundation of the general government. Until these States had formed their constitutions, there was no republican government in the world except Switzerland and San Marino, and these lived only on the sufferance of their powerful monarchical neighbors. All South America

---

* One of our most distinguished citizens said some years ago that he believed the tendency of things was towards the English language, the Christian religion, and republican government for the human race.

was under Spanish rule, and Mexico was a monarchy.

The great principle of a republic is that people *have a right to choose* their own rulers, and ought to do it. The divine right of hereditary monarchy we deny. It is often said that the English government is as free as ours; but it is not quite true, and will not be true until every citizen is permitted to vote for his rulers. Whether so much liberty is perfectly safe for all people is well open to question; but it is a FACT here, and if people would only behave themselves properly there would be no danger whatever in it. And if there IS danger here, it comes not from native-born citizens trained under our free institutions. The sun does not shine on a broader, fairer land than this; and under that divine Providence, without whose gracious aid we could not have achieved and cannot maintain our Constitution, we have nothing whatever to fear for the present or to dread in the future, but the evil men among us—the Anarchists and Socialists, the scum and off-scouring of Europe—who, with no fear of God before their eyes, so far forget the high aims of this government and their own obligations to it as to seek to overthrow its very foundations.

The highest and best types of monarchical governments are in Europe, and it is with such that we seek comparison when we insist that ours is better.

Monarchies are hereditary. They descend from

father to the oldest son and to the oldest son of the oldest son where there are sons. England has rejoiced in two female sovereigns at least, Elizabeth, and Victoria, the present sovereign; but they came to the throne because there was no son in either case to inherit. The heir-apparent, whatever his character or want of character, MUST reign when the sovereign dies, because, as they say, he rules by divine right. We insist on electing our President for a term of years, and if we like him we give him another term; if we do not like him, we drop him and try another. I wish the term of office of the President were longer, and that he could serve only one term. Perhaps it will come to that; and I think he would be a more independent, a better official under this condition.

What is the difference between the Constitution and the laws?

The Constitution is the great charter under which, and within which, the laws are made. No law that Congress may pass is worth the paper it is printed on if it is contrary to the Constitution. Such laws have been passed ignorantly, and have died.

A very simple illustration is at hand. The constitution of this College is Mr. Girard's will. This is our charter. The laws which the Directors make must be within the provisions of the will or they will not stand. For instance, the will directs that none but *orphans* can be admitted here; and the courts have decided that a child without a father is an orphan.

The Directors, therefore, cannot admit the child who has a father living. The will says that only *boys* can be admitted; therefore no law that the Directors can make will admit a girl. Nor can the Directors make a law which will admit a colored boy; nor a boy under six nor over ten years of age; nor a boy born anywhere except in certain States of our country— Pennsylvania, New York and Louisiana. It would be UNCONSTITUTIONAL. I think now you see the difference between the Constitution and the laws.

Now, again, is our government better than a monarchy? and why?

Because the men of the present time make it, and are not bound by the traditions of far-off times. There are improvements in the science of government as in all other human inventions, as the centuries come and go. Man is progressive; he would not be worth caring for if he were not. If the present age has not produced a higher and better development in all essentials, it is our own fault, and is not because men were perfect in the past or cannot be better in the present or in the future. Therefore when our Constitution is believed not to meet the requirements of the present day there is a way to amend it, although that way is so hedged up that it cannot possibly be altered without ample time for consideration. As a matter ot fact, the Constitution has been altered or amended fifteen times since its adoption; and it will be changed or amended as often as the needs of the people require it.

We believe our form of government to be better than any monarchy because *the people choose their own law-makers*. The Congress is composed of two houses or chambers: the members of the Senate, chosen by the legislatures of the States, two from each State, to serve for six years; the members of the House of Representatives (chosen by the citizens), who sit for two years only, unless re-elected. The Senate is supposed to be the more conservative body, not easily moved by popular clamor; while the Representatives, chosen directly and recently by the voters, are supposed to know the immediate wants of the people. The thought of two houses grew probably from the two houses of the British parliament.

We cannot have an *hereditary legislature* like the House of Lords in the British parliament, whose members sit, as the sovereign rules, by divine right, as they say, and with the same result in some instances: for the sovereign may be a mere figure-head, or only the nominal ruler, while the cabinet is the real government, and the House of Lords long ago sunk far below the House of Commons in real influence. There is no better reason for this than the fact that the people have nothing to do with the House of Lords and the sovereign, except to depose and scatter them when they choose to rise in their power and assert themselves.

We can have no *orders of nobility* under our Constitution. There can be no privileged class. All men are equal under the law. I do not mean that all persons are equal in all respects. Divine Providence has made us unequal. Some are endowed naturally with the highest mental and physical gifts and distinctions; some are strong and others weak. This has always been so and always will be so. Some have inherited or acquired riches, while others have to labor diligently to make a bare living. Some have inherited their high culture and gentle manners and noble instincts, which, in a general sense, we sometimes call culture; and others have to acquire all this for themselves—and it is not very easy to get it. So there is no such thing as absolute equality, and cannot be; but before the law, in the enjoyment of our rights and in the undisturbed possession of what we have, we are all equal, as we could not be under a monarchy. Here there is no legal bar to success; all places are open to all.

There can be no law of *primogeniture* under our Constitution. By this law, which still prevails in England, the eldest son inherits the titles and estates of the father, while the younger sons and all the daughters must be provided for in other ways. Some of the sons are put in the church, in the army or the navy, or in the professions, such as law and medicine; but it is very rare indeed that any son of a noble house is willing to engage in any kind of business or trade, for they are not so well thought of if they become tradesmen.

There can be no *state church*, no *establishment*, under our Constitution. In England the Episcopal Church, and in Scotland the Presbyterian Church, are established by law; and until within the last seventeen years the Church of England was by law established in Ireland; and it is now established in Wales; and in other countries of Europe the Roman Catholic Church and the Lutheran Church and the Greek Church are established by law. In countries where there is a national church, it derives more or less of its support from taxing the people, many of whom do not belong to it; but in this land there is no established church; and there never can be, let us hope and believe.

Under our form of government we need no *standing army*. We owe this partly to the fact that we are so isolated geographically that we do not need to keep an army. I heard the general of our army say, a short time ago, that the regular army of the United States is a fiction—only 25,000 men. (You saw as many troops a few weeks ago in one day as are in all our army.) "The real army," he added, "is composed of every able-bodied citizen; for all are ready to volunteer in the face of a common enemy." Our territory is immensely large already, and it will probably be larger, but it will not again be enlarged as the result of war. When we look at the nations of Europe, and see the immense numbers of men in their standing armies, we can't help thanking God that we are separated from them by the wide Atlantic, and that we have a republican government, and have no temptation to seek other territory, and are not likely to be attacked for any cause. In the armies of Great Britain, Germany, Russia, Austria, Italy, Turkey, are more than ten millions of men withdrawn from the cultivation of the soil and from the pursuits of commerce and manufactures. In Italy alone the standing army is said to be 750,000 men! The withdrawal of so many men from peaceful occupations makes it necessary to employ women to do work which in our country women are never asked to do. I have seen a woman drawing a boat on a canal, and a man sitting on the deck of that boat smoking his pipe and steering the boat. I have seen a woman with a huge load of fresh hay upon her head and a man walking by her side and carrying his scythe. I have seen women yoked with dogs to carts, carrying the loads that here would be put in a cart and drawn by a horse. I have seen women carrying the hod for masons on their *heads*, filled with stone and mortar. I have seen women carrying huge baskets of manure on their backs to the field, and young girls breaking stone on the highway. Did you ever hear of such things here? See what a difference! The men in the army eat up the substance which the women produce from the soil.

But nowhere else in the world is the *dignity of labor* recognized as here. They do not know the meaning of the words. For in most other countries it is considered undignified, if not ungenteel, to be engaged in labor of any kind. A man who is not able to live without work is hardly considered a gentleman. To work with the hands is degrading; is what ought to be done by common people only, and by people who are not fit to associate with gentlemen and ladies. It is not so in this country. Here, a man who is well educated and well behaved, and upright and honorable in his dealings with men, who cultivates his mind by reading and observation, and is careful of the usages of good society, is fit company for any one. He may rise to any place within the gift of his fellow-citizens, and adorn it. This is not so elsewhere. And think of a young girl hardly out of her teens, with no special preparation for such a distinction, but educated and accomplished, becoming the wife of the President of the United States, and proving herself entirely worthy of that high position! Could any other country match this?

Now what is the effect of all this freedom of thought and action on the people? Well, it is not to be denied that there are some disadvantages. There is danger that we may over-estimate the individual in his personal rights, and not give due weight to the people as a community. There is danger of selfishness, especially among young people. There is not as much respect and reverence for age, and for those above us, and for the other sex, as there ought to be. Young people are very rude at times, when they should always be polite to their superiors in age or position. At a little city in Bavaria the boys coming out of school one day all lifted their hats to me, a stranger! That would be an astounding thing in a Philadelphia street! In riding in the neighborhood of the city here, if I speak civilly to a boy by the roadside, I am just as likely as not to get an impudent answer.

But in spite of these defects, which we hope will never be seen in a Girard College boy, the true effect of training under our republican institutions is to make men. There is a wider, freer, fuller development of what is in man than is known elsewhere. Man is much more likely to become self-reliant, self-dependent, vigorous, skillful, here—not knowing how high he may rise, and consciously or unconsciously preparing himself for anything to which he may be called. And for woman, too, where else does she meet the respect that belongs to her? Where else in the world do women find occupation in government offices, on school boards, at the head of charitable and educational institutions? With few exceptions, such as Girton College, where are there in any other country such colleges as Vassar or Wellesley, and as the Woman's Medical College, almost under the walls of our own?

I have already kept you too long. But a few words and I am done. I am moved by the injunction of Mr. Girard in his will not only to say these things, but by this grave consideration also. Every boy who hears me to-day, within fifteen years, if he lives, unless he is cut off by crime from the privilege, will be a voter. You will go to the polls to cast your votes for those who are to have the conduct of the government in all its parts. I want to make you feel, if I can, the high destiny that awaits you. You are distinctive in this respect—you are all American boys. This can be said of no other assembly as large as this in all this broad land. You have it in your power, and I want to help you to it, and God will if you ask him—you have it in your power to become American gentlemen. And I believe that an *American gentleman* is the very highest type of man.

> God, give us men. A time like this demands
> Strong minds, great hearts, true faith and ready hands:
> Men whom the lust of office does not kill;
>    Men whom the spoils of office cannot buy;
> Men who possess opinions and a will;
>    Men who have honor, men who will not lie;
> Men who can stand before a demagogue
>    And scorn his treacherous flatteries without winking;
> Tall men, sun-crowned, who live above the fog
>    In public duty and in private thinking.

## JAMES LAWRENCE CLAGHORN.

When a man has lived a long, busy, useful and successful life it seems proper that something more than the ordinary obituary notices in the daily papers is due to his memory. This thought moves me to speak to you to-day of a gentleman who died on August 25, 1884, while a Director of the Girard College, and of whom it seems appropriate that something may be said to you in this chapel.

Mr. James L. Claghorn was a distinguished citizen of Philadelphia. He was born here on the 5th of July, 1817. His father, John W. Claghorn, was a merchant of excellent standing, who in the latter years of his life gave much time and thought to benevolent institutions. At the age of fourteen years James left school to go into business. You boys know how very incomplete an education at school must be which ends when the boy is fourteen years old. But you don't know until your own experience proves it how hard it is for a half-educated boy to compete for the high places in life or in business with boys of equal natural ability, who have had the full advantage of a liberal school education. At fourteen, then, James Claghorn turned his back on school and went to work in earnest. For it was an auction store that he entered, and the work there was usually harder work than in other kinds of stores. The hours of labor were longer—earlier and later—and the holidays more rare than in ordinary commercial houses.

There is no record of the early years of his business life; but it is not difficult to imagine the hardships to which a young lad of that time would be subjected. We can't suppose that any indulgence was allowed him because his father was one of the partners in the firm; neither he nor his father would have permitted such distinction.

The boy must have been *industrious;* for in such a house there was no place for an idle lounger. He was not afraid of work, for he was always at it; he did not spare himself, else some other boy would have done his share and got ahead of him; he must have been *faithful*, not one who works only when his master's eye is on him—not shirking any hard work—not forgetting to-day what he was told yesterday—not thinking too much of his rights or his own particular work, but doing anything that came to hand—looking always to the interest of the firm, and trusting the future for a recognition of his faithfulness.

And he must have been *patient*. Many rough

words, many hasty and passionate words are spoken to young boys, and must have been spoken to this boy, and may have hurt him; but there is good reason to believe from the character he built up that he knew how to hold his tongue and not answer back. Not every boy has learned that useful lesson; and hence the many outbreaks of passion and the frequent discharge of boys who will "answer back" when they are reproved.

And I think also that he must have been of a bright and cheery disposition and well mannered. Some young fellows who have to make their way in the world seem not to know the importance of a good address; in other words, politeness, good breeding. Nothing impresses one so favorably at first meeting a stranger as good manners. A frank, hearty greeting, a bright, cheerful face, a manly bearing, a willingness to consider others, a desire to please for the sake of giving pleasure, are of great importance. On the contrary, sullenness, sluggishness, indifference, selfishness are all repulsive, and though allowance will be made at first for the existence of such qualities, yet they will hardly be tolerated long in a young person, and they will certainly unfit him for a successful career. I did not know Mr. Claghorn when he was a young lad; but I can hardly suppose that the kindly, genial, hearty man in middle and later life could have been a morose, sullen, sluggish, ill-mannered boy.

I have said that Mr. Claghorn left school while still a boy; but we must not infer that he supposed his education was complete with the end of his school life, for it is very evident that he must have given very much of his leisure to self-improvement. We do not know how his evenings were spent when not in the counting-house; but he must have given a good deal of time to reading; and it is not likely that the books which he read were such as are to be found now at any book-stand, and in the hands of so many boys as they go to and fro on their errands—books which are simply read without instruction, and which sometimes treat of subjects which are unreal, extravagant, coarse and brutalizing. Doubtless he was fond of fiction. All boys of fair education and refined taste are more or less fond of fiction; but we can hardly suppose that he gave too much of his time to such reading, else he could not have become the strong business man that he was. At a very early age he became fond of art, and gathered about him as his means would permit engravings and pictures such as would cultivate his taste in that direction. When he could spare the money he would buy an engraving, if the subject or the author interested him; so that he became, in the latter part of his life, the owner of one of the largest collections of engravings in the whole country. Indeed, he became a noted patron of art, and especially was he desirous of encouraging *native* art, so that at one period he had more than two hundred paintings, the work of American artists; for at that time he was more desirous of encouraging native artists, especially if they were poor, than he was in making collections of the great masters. Many a picture he bought to help the artist, rather than for his own gratification as a collector. Further on in life he became deeply interested in the Academy of the Fine Arts, which was then in Chestnut street above Tenth. Subsequently he became its President, and very largely through his influence and his personal means that fine building at the southwest corner of Broad and Cherry street, which all of you ought to visit as opportunity is afforded, was erected as a depository of art. The splendid building of the Academy of Music at Broad and Locust street, is also largely indebted to Mr. Claghorn for its erection.

But I am anticipating, and we must now go back to Mr. Claghorn in his counting-house. No longer a boy—an apprentice—he has grown to manhood, and has become a member of the firm, taking his father's place. Now his labors are greatly increased; the hours of business, which were long before, are longer now; he begins very early in the morning, before sunrise in the winter season, and is sometimes detained late in the evening, the long day being entirely devoted to business; and no one knows, except one who has gone through that sort of experience, how much labor is involved in such a life; but not only his labors—his responsibilities are greatly increased. He becomes the financial man in the firm; he is the head of the counting-house; he has charge of the books and the accounts. For many years no entry was made in the huge ledgers except in his own handwriting. The credit of the house of Myers & Claghorn becomes deservedly high. A time of great financial excitement and distress comes on. This house, while others are going down on the right and left like ships in a storm, stands erect with unimpaired credit, and with opportunities of helping other and weaker houses which so much needed help. The name of his firm was a synonym of all that is strong and admirable in business management.

So he passed the best years of his whole life in earnest attention to business, snatching all the leisure he could for the gratification of his passion, it may be called, for art, until the time came when, having acquired what was at that time supposed to be an abundant competency, he determined to retire from business. Now he appears to contemplate a long rest in a visit to other countries, and was making arrangements looking to a long holiday of great enjoyment, when the country became involved in the Great Rebellion. None of you, except as you read it in history, know what a convulsion passed over the country when the first gun was fired upon the flag at Fort Sumter. Mr. Claghorn, full of love for his country and unwilling to do what seemed to him almost like a desertion in her time of trial, gave up his contemplated foreign tour, and applied himself most diligently and earnestly to the duties of a true, loyal citizen in the support of the government. He was one of the earliest members of the Union League, and was largely interested in collecting money for the raising and equipping of regiments to be sent to the front. Three or four years of his life were spent in this laudable work, and in company with those of like mind he was largely instrumental in accomplishing great good. The war, however, came to an end—was fought out to its final and inevitable issue.

Now the desire to visit foreign countries returned with increased interest. His business affairs, although they had not been as profitable as they would have been if he had looked closer to them and had given less thought to public matters during the war, were so satisfactory that he could afford to put them in other hands for a while, and in company with his wife he embarked for Europe. It was to be a long holiday such as he had never known before. He intended to make an extended tour—he was not to be hurried. He went through England, Scotland, Ireland, France, Switzerland, Spain, Italy, Egypt, Palestine, Turkey, Greece, Austria, Russia, Germany, Holland and Belgium. In this way he saw and enjoyed all the most famous picture-galleries of the old world; and his long study of art in its various phases and schools gave him special advantages for the highest enjoyment of the great collections, public and private, of the old masters as well as of those of modern times.

The interest of his extended tour was not, however, limited to galleries and collections of paintings and statuary. He was an observer of men and things. His practical American mind observed and digested everything that came within his reach. The government of the great cities—the condition of the masses of the people gathered in them—the common people outside of the cities, their customs and costumes; their way of living—in short, everything that was unlike what we see at home—he observed and remembered to enjoy in the retrospect of after years.

It was hardly to be expected that Mr. Claghorn, having lived the busy life that he had lived before he went abroad, should have been content on his return to sit down in the enjoyment of his well-earned leisure; and accordingly, shortly after his return, he became the President of the Commercial National Bank, one of the oldest financial institutions in our city. For several years previously he had been a Director in the Philadelphia National Bank (as his father had before him), so that he had had proper training for the duties of his new position. He became also a Manager in the Philadelphia Saving Fund Society, the oldest and the largest saving fund in our city. With most commendable diligence and industry he at once set about building up the bank so as to make it profitable to its stockholders. Not forgetting, however, the attractions of art, he covered the walls of his bank parlor with beautiful specimens of the choicest engravings, so that even the daily routine of business life might be enlivened by glimpses into the attractive world of art.

In the year 1869, when the Board of City Trusts was created by act of Legislature (to which board is committed the vast estate left by Mr. Girard, as well as of the other trusts of the city of Philadelphia), Mr. Claghorn was appointed one of the original board of twelve, and from that date until his death he gave much time and thought to the duties thus devolved upon him. He became chairman of the finance committee, which place he held until the end of his life. Although he was not so well known to the boys of the college as some other members of this board, because his duties did not require very frequent visits to the college, he nevertheless gave himself to the duties of the committee of which he was chairman with great interest and fidelity; and the time which he gave to this great work is not to be measured by visits to the college, but by the time spent in the city office and in his own place of business, where his committee met him on their stated meetings. As I have reason to know, he had a deep personal interest in all the affairs of this college, and of the other trusts committed to our charge.

Although the condition of his health in the latter part of his life made close attention to business very trying to him, so far as I know he never permitted his health to interfere with his business engagements.

In this brief and fragmentary way I have tried to set before you some features of the life of one of our most distinguished citizens. In the limits of a single discourse as brief as this must be it is not possible to make this more than an outline sketch. In the little time that remains let me refer again for the purpose of emphasis to some traits in the character of Mr. Claghorn which will justly bear reconsideration.

A very large proportion of the merchants of any city fail in business. The proportion is much larger than is generally known, and larger than young people are willing to believe.

In an experience of more than forty years of business life, during which I have had much to do with merchants, I have known so many failures, have seen so many wrecks of commercial houses, that I am compelled to regard a merchant who has maintained high credit for a long term of years and finally retired from business with a handsome estate as one who is entitled to the respect and confidence of his fellow-citizens. Some men grow rich as junior partners in successful business, the good management having been due to the ability and tact of their seniors; but this can hardly be said in the present case. The merchant whose life we are considering was an active and influential partner.

Let me say, however, that true success in business is not to be measured by the amount of money one accumulates. A man may be rich in the riches acquired by his own activity and shrewdness who is in no high sense a successful business man. These things are necessary: He should be a just man, an upright, honorable man, a man of breadth and solidity of character, who gathers about him some of the ablest and best of his fellow-citizens in labors for the good of others and the welfare of society. In such sense was Mr. Claghorn a successful business man.

His early love of art in its various forms, the substantial aid and encouragement he gave to young students in their beginnings, his deep sympathy with persons who in literature and art were striving for a living, his generous hospitality to artists, and his public spirit—all these had their influence in the growth and development of his character, and made his name to be loved and honored by many who shared in his generous sympathies.

Mr. Claghorn's love of country, which we call patriotism, was signally disclosed at the outbreak of the war in 1861. When we remember his long and busy life as a merchant—broken by few or no vacations such as most other men enjoyed—when we remember that his self-culture had been of such a nature as to prepare him most admirably well for a tour in foreign countries, especially such countries as had produced the ablest, the most distinguished artists—we can have some idea of what it cost him to forego the much needed rest—to deny himself the well-earned pleasure of a visit to the picture galleries of Europe, where are gathered the treasures of the highest art in all the world. Many men in like circumstances would have felt that one man, whose age and sedentary habits unfitted him for active service in the field, would hardly be missed from among the loyal citizens of the North—but he did not think so; and therefore he put aside all his personal plans, and in the city where he was born he remained and devoted himself as one of her true, loyal citizens in raising money and men for the defence of the government. There could be no truer heroism than this, and right bravely and successfully he carried his purpose to the end.

"I am permitted," said the clergyman who spoke at his funeral, and with his words I close these remarks, "I am permitted to address to you in the presence of the solemnity of death some few reflections that occur to me in memory of one whom we shall know no more in life. A few Saturday evenings ago I was walking along by a lake at a seashore home when a great and wondrous beauty spread itself beneath my eye. It was one of those inimitable pictures that rarely come to one. In the foreground there lay a lake with no ripple on its surface. It was a calm and sleeping thing. A shining glory was in the western sky. The sun had gone, but where he disappeared were indications of beauty—one of the most beautiful afterglows I have ever seen. It was not one of the ordinary things, and as I looked at it there came many reflections. Here is one of them. It seems quite applicable this morning. That which caused the quiet glory of the lake, that which caused the radiation of beauty, had gone. Its day's work was done. That quiet lake and streaked sky were the type of a picture of a busy, useful, successful life that had been accomplished. It was a complete thing. The day was done. The activity had passed away. It was finished just as this life. What had made it beautiful had gone, but he flung back monuments of beauty that made the scene as beautiful as good words and noble deeds make the memory of man. There were six of these rays. Young men, brethren of this community, you will do well to remember that anywhere and everywhere, without patience and industry, nothing great can be done. The life departed was a busy one—one of busy usefulness. The cry that came from him was, 'I must work; I must be busy.' Live as this man did, that your life may be one that can be held up as an example and a light to young men of the coming generations. One ray of beauty was his sterling truthfulness. It is a splendid thing to be trusted by your fellows. Another ray was his prudent foresight. It was characteristic of him, and it is a splendid thing to have. Another ray that welled out of him was his striking humanity. There was one continual trait in his character. I would call it manhoodness. There was another feature—his deep humility."

Such were some of the traits of character of a man who lived a long life in the city where he was born. If no distinctive monument has been erected to his memory, there are the "Union League," "The Academy of the Fine Arts," and "The Academy of Music," with which his name will always be associated; and, what is better still, there are many hearts that throb with grateful memories of an unselfish man, who in time of sore need stretched out his hand to help, and that hand was never empty. And you will remember, you Girard boys, that this man who did so much for his native city and for his fellow-citizens was not nearly so well educated at the age of fourteen when he left school as many of you are now. See what he did; see what some of you may do!

# THE LEAF TURNED OVER.

January 1, 1888.

SOME weeks ago I gave you two lectures on "Turning Over a New Leaf." One of the directors of this college to whom I sent a printed copy said I ought to follow those with another on this subject: "The Leaf Turned Over." I at once accepted this suggestion and shall now try to follow his advice.

Most thoughtful people as they approach the end of a year are apt to ask themselves some plain questions—as to their manner of life, their habits of thought, their amusements, their studies, their business, their home, their families, their companions, their plans for the future, their duty to their fellowmen, their duty to God; in short, whether the year about to close has been a happy one; whether they have been successful or otherwise in what they have attempted to do.

The merchant, manufacturer or man of business of any kind who keeps books, and whose accounts are properly kept, looks with great interest at his account book at such a time, to see whether his businer has been profitable or otherwise, whether he has lost or made money, whether his capital is larger or smaller than it was at the beginning of the year, whether he is solvent or insolvent, whether he is able to pay his debts or is bankrupt.

And to very many persons engaged in business for themselves, this is a time of great anxiety, for one can hardly tell exactly whether he is getting on favorably until his account books are posted and the balances are struck. If one's capital is small and the result of the year's business is a loss, that means a reduction of capital, and raises the question whether this can go on for some years without failure and bankruptcy. Many and many a business man looks with great anxiety to the month of December, and especially to the end of it, to learn whether he shall be able to go on in his business, however humble. And, alas! there are many whose books of account are so badly kept, and whose balances are so rarely struck, or who keep no account books at all, that they never know how they stand, but are always under the apprehension that any day they may fail to meet their obligations and so fail and become bankrupt. They were insolvent long before, but they did not know it; and they have gone on from bad to worse until they are ruined. Others, again, are afraid to look closely into their account books—afraid to have the balances struck, lest they should be convinced that their affairs are in a hopeless condition. Unhappy cowards they are, for if insolvent the sooner they know it the better, that they may make the best settlement they can with their creditors, if the business is worth following at all, and begin again, "turning over a new leaf."

I do not suppose that many of you boys have ever thought much on these subjects; for you are not in business as principals or as clerks, you have no merchandise or produce or money to handle, you have no account books for yourselves or for other people to keep, to post, to balance, and you may think you have no interest in these remarks; but I hope to be able to show you that these things are not matters of indifference to you.

The year 1887, which closed last night, was just as much *your* year as it was that of any man, even the busiest man of affairs. When it came, 365 days ago, it found you (most of you) at school here: it left all of you here. And the question naturally arises, what have you done with this time, all these days and nights? Every page in the account books of certain kinds of business represents a day of business, and either the figures on both the debit and the credit side are added up and carried forward, or the balance of the two sides of the page is struck and carried over leaf to the next page.

So every day of the past year represents a page in the history of your lives: for every life, even the plainest and most humble, has its own peculiar history. Your lives here are uneventful; no very startling things occur to break the monotony of school life, but each day has its own duties and makes its own record. Three hundred and sixty-five pages of the book of the history of every young life here were duly filled by the records of all the things done or neglected, of the words spoken or unspoken, of the thoughts indulged or stifled; these pages with their records, sad or joyful, glad or shameful, were turned over, and are now numbered with the things that are past and gone. When an accountant or book-keeper discovers, after the books of the year are closed and the balances struck, that errors had crept in which have disturbed the accuracy of his work, he cannot go back with a knife and erase the errors and write in the correct figures; neither can he blot them out, nor rub them out as you do examples from a slate or from the blackboard; he must correct his mistakes; he must counteract his blunders by new entries on a new page.

It is somewhat so with us, with you. Last night at midnight the last page of the leaves of the book of the old year was filled with its record, whatever it was, and this morning "the leaf is turned over." What do we see? What does every one of you see? A fair, white page. And each one of you holds a pen in his hand and the inkstand is within reach; you dip your pen in the ink, you bend over the page, the thoughts come thick and fast, much faster indeed than any pen, even that of the quickest shorthand writer can put them on the page. There are stenographers who can take the language of the most rapid speakers, but no stenographer has ever yet appeared who can put his own thoughts on paper as rapidly as they come into his mind. But while there is but one mind in all the universe that can have knowledge of what is passing in your mind and retain it all—THE INFINITE MIND; and while no one page of any book, however large, even if it be what bookmakers call elephant folio, can possibly hold the record of what any boy here says and thinks in a single day, you may, and you do, all of you, write words good or bad on the page before you.

Let me take one of these boys not far from the desk, a boy of sixteen or seventeen years of age, who is now waiting, pen in hand, to write the thoughts now passing in his mind. What are these thoughts? No one knows but himself. Shall I tell you what I think he ought to write? It is something like this:

"I have been here many years. When I came I was young and ignorant. I found myself among many boys of my own age, hardly any of whom I ever saw before, who cared no more for me than I cared for them. I felt very strange; the first few days and nights I was very unhappy, for I missed very much my mother and the others whom I had left at home. But very soon these feelings passed away. I was put to school at once, and in the school-room and the play-ground I soon forgot the things and the people about my other home. Years passed. I was promoted from one school to another, from one section to another; I grew rapidly in size; my classmates were no longer little boys; we were all looking up and looking forward to the school promotions, and I became a big boy. The lessons were hard, and I studied hard, for I began to understand at last why I was sent here, and to ask myself the question, what might reasonably be expected of me? Sometimes when quite alone this question would force itself upon me, what use am I making of my fine advantages, or am I making the best use of them? And what manner of man shall I be? For I know full well that all well-educated boys do not succeed in life—do not become successful men in the highest and best sense. How do I know that I shall do well? Is my conduct here such as to justify the authorities in commending me as a thoroughly manly, trustworthy boy? Have I succeeded while going through the course of school studies in building up a character that is worthy of me, worthy of this great school? Can those who know me best place the most confidence in me? If I am looking forward to a place in a machine shop, or in a store, or in a lawyer's office, or to the study of medicine, or to a place in a railroad office or a bank, am I really trying to fit myself for such a place, or am I simply drifting along from day to day, doing only what I am compelled to do and cultivating no true ambition to rise above the dull average of my companions? And then, as I look at the difficulties in the way of every young fellow who has his way to make in the world, has it not occurred to me to look beyond the present and the persons and things that surround me now, and look to a higher and better Helper than is to be found in this world? Have I not at times heard words of good counsel in this chapel, from the lips of those who come to give me and my companions wholesome advice? What attention have I given to such advice? I have been told, and I do not doubt it, that the great God stoops from heaven and speaks to my soul, and offers his Divine help, and even holds out his hand, though I cannot see it, and will take my hand in his, and help me over all hard places, and will never let me go, if I cling to him, and will assure me success in everything that is right and good. I have heard all this over and over again; I know it is true, but I have not accepted it as if I believed it; I have not acted accordingly; in fact, I have treated the whole matter as if it were unreal, or as if it referred to somebody else rather than to me.

"And now I have come probably to my last year in this school. Before another New Year's day some other boy will have my desk in the school-room, my bed in the dormitory, my place at the table, my seat in the chapel. These long years, oh! how long they have seemed, have nearly all passed; I shall soon go away; if some place is not found for me I must find one for myself—oh! what will become of me? Since last New Year's day two boys who were educated here have been sent convicted criminals to the Eastern Penitentiary. What are they thinking about on this New Year's morning? They sat on these seats, they sang our hymns, they heard the same good words of advice which I have heard, they had all the good opportunities which all of us have; what led them astray? Did they believe that the good God stooped from heaven to say good words to them, holding out his strong hand to help them? I wonder if they thought they were strong enough to take care of themselves? I wonder if they thought they could get along without his help? Do I think I can?"

Some such thoughts as these may be passing in the mind of the boy now looking at me and sitting not far from the desk, the boy whom I had in my mind as I began to speak. He is holding his pen full of ink. He has written nothing yet; he has been listening with some curiosity to hear what the speaker will say, what he can possibly know of a boy's thoughts.

I can tell that boy what *I* would write if I were at his age, in this college, and surrounded by these circumstances, listening to these serious, earnest words. I would take my pen and write on the first page of this year's book, this Sunday morning, this New Year's day, these words: "*The leaf is turned over!*

## THE LEAF TURNED OVER. 151

God help me to lead a better life. God forgive all the past, all my wrong doings, all my neglect, all my forgetfulness. God keep me in right ways. God keep me from wicked thoughts which defile the soul; keep me from wicked words which defile the souls of others."

"But this is a prayer," you say; "do you want me to begin my journal by writing a prayer?"

Yes; but this is not all. Write again.

1. *I will not willingly break any of the rules which are adopted for the government of our school.*

Some of the rules may *seem* hard to obey, and even unreasonable, but they were made for my good by those who are wiser than I am. I *can* obey them; I *will*.

2. *I will work harder over my lessons than ever before, and I will recite them more accurately.*

This means hard work, but it is my duty; I shall be the better for it; it will not be long, for I am going soon; I *can*, I *will*.

3. *I will watch my thoughts and my talk more carefully than I have ever done before.*

If I have hurt others by evil talk I will do so no more. It is a common fault; many of us boys have fallen into the habit of it; but for one, I will do so no more; I *can* stop it, I *will*.

4. *I will be more careful in my daily life here, to set a good example in all things, than I have ever been before.*

The younger boys look to the older boys and imitate them closely. They watch us, our words, our ways, our behavior in all things. If any young fellows have been misled by me, it shall be so no more. I will behave so that no one shall be the worse for doing as I do. This is quite within my control; I *can*, I *will*.

5. *I will look to God to help me to do these things.*

For I have tried to do something like this before and failed; it must be because I depended on my own strength. Now I will look away from myself and depend upon "God, without whom nothing is strong, nothing is holy." He *can* help me; he surely will, if I throw myself on his mercy, and by daily prayer and reading the Scriptures, even if only for a moment or two each day, I shall see light and find peace.

These are the things that I would write, my boy, if I were just as you are.

Shall I stop now? May I not go a little farther and say some words to others here?

Teachers, prefects, governesses: these boys are all under your charge, and every day. The same good Providence that brought them here for education and support, brought you here also to teach them and care for them. Your work is exacting, laborious, unremitting. Some of these young boys are trying to your patience, your temper, your forbearance, almost beyond endurance. Sometimes you are discouraged by what seems to be the almost hopeless nature of your work, the untidiness, the rough manners, the ill temper, the stupidity of some of these young boys. But remember that all this is inevitable; that from the nature of the case it must be so; and remember, too, that to reduce such material to good order, to train and educate these young lives so that they shall be well educated, well informed, well mannered, polite, gentle, considerate, so they may be fairly well assured of a successful future, is a great and noble work, worthy of the ambition of the highest intelligence. This is exactly what the great founder had in his mind when he established this college and provided so munificently for its endowment. This is what his trustees most earnestly desire, and the hope of which rewards them for the many hours they give every week to the care of this great estate. We depend upon you to carry out the plan of instruction here, not only in the schools, but in the section rooms and on the play-grounds. Be to these older boys their big brothers, their best friends. Be kind to them always, even when compelled to reprove them for their many faults.

And to those of you who have the care of the younger boys, let me say: remember, they have no mothers here; they are very young to send from home; they are homesick at times; they hardly know how to behave themselves; they shock your sense of delicacy; they worry and vex you almost to distraction; but bear with them, help them, encourage them, love them, for if *you* do not, who will? And what will become of them? And remember what a glorious work it is to lift such a young life out of its rudeness, its ignorance, its untidiness, and make a real man of it. Oh! friends, suffer these words of exhortation, for they come from one who has a deep sympathy with you in your arduous, self-denying work.

And I saw a great white throne, and him that sat on it from whose face the earth and the heaven fled away; and there was found no place for them. And I saw the dead, small and great, stand before God; and the books were opened; and another book was opened, which is the book of life; and the dead were judged out of those things which were written in the books, according to their works. And the sea gave up the dead that were in it; and death and hell delivered up the dead which were in them; and they were judged every man according to his works — Rev. xx. 11–13.

# THANKSGIVING DAY.

November 29, 1888.

THE President of the United States, in a proclamation which you have just heard, has set apart this 29th day of November for a day of thanksgiving and prayer, for the great mercies which the Almighty has given to the people of our country, and for a continuance of these mercies. His example has been followed by the governors of Pennsylvania and many, if not all, of the States, and we may therefore believe that all over the land, from Maine to Alaska, and from the great lakes to the Gulf of Mexico, the people in large numbers are now gathered or gathering in their places of worship, in obedience to this proper recommendation. The directors of this college, in full sympathy with the thoughts of our rulers, have closed your schools to-day, released you from the duty of study, gathered you in this chapel, and asked you to unite with the people generally in giving thanks to God for the past, and imploring his mercies for the future. For you are a part of the people, and although not yet able, from your minority, to take an active part in the government, are yet being rapidly prepared for this great right of citizenship. It is the high privilege of an American boy, to know that when he becomes a man he will have just as clear a right as any other man, to exercise all the functions of a freeman, in choosing the men who are to be intrusted with the responsibilities of government. What are some of the things that give us cause for thankfulness to Almighty God? Very briefly such as these:

1. *This is a Christian country.* Although there is not, and cannot be, any part or branch of the church established by law, there is assured liberty for every citizen to worship God by himself, or with others in congregations, as he or they may choose, in such forms of worship as may be preferred, with none to molest or make afraid. Here is absolute freedom of worship. And even if it be that the name of God is not in our Constitution, nevertheless no president or governor or public officer can be inducted or inaugurated in high office except by taking oath on the book of God, and as in his presence, that he will faithfully discharge the duties of his office. If there were nothing else, this public acknowledgment of the being of Almighty God and our accountability to him gives us an unquestioned right to call ourselves a Christian people.

2. *This is a free government*, free in the sense that the people choose their own rulers, whether of towns, cities, States, or the nation. There is no hereditary

rule here, and cannot be. We not only *choose* our own rulers, but when we are dissatisfied with them for whatever cause, we dismiss them. And the minority accept the decision when it is ascertained, without doubt, without a question of its righteousness; they only want to know whether the majority have actually chosen this or that candidate, and they accept frankly, if not cheerfully. We have had a splendid illustration of this within this present month. The great party that has administered the government for four years past, on the verdict of the majority, are preparing to retire and will retire on the fourth of March next, and give up the government to the other great party, its victorious rival. Nowhere else in the world can such a revolution be accomplished on so grand a scale, by so many people, with so little friction. This government then is better than *any monarchy*, no matter how carefully guarded by constitutional restrictions and safeguards. The best monarchical governments are in Europe: the best of all in England; but the governments of Europe have many and great concessions to make to the people, before they can stand side by side with the United States in strong, healthy, considerate management of the people. It has been said that the best machinery is that which has the least friction, and as the time passes, we may hope that our machinery of government will be so smooth that the people will hardly know that they are governed at all; in fact, they will be their own governors. This time is coming as sure as Christmas, though not so close at hand, and you boys can hasten it by your own upright, manly bearing when you come to be men. Never forget that this is a government of the majority, and you must see to it that the majority be true men.

3. *We are separated by wide oceans from tne rest of the world.* The Atlantic separates us from Europe on the east; the Gulf of Mexico from South America on the south, and the great Pacific ocean washes our western shores. We are a continent to ourselves, with the exception of Mexico, a sister republic on the south, with whom we are not likely to quarrel again, and the Dominion of Canada on the north, which, if never to become a part of ourselves, will at least at some day, and probably not a very distant day, become independent of the mother country as we did, though not at the great cost at which we obtained our freedom. Our distance from Europe relieves us entirely from the consideration of subjects which occupy most of the time of their statesmen, and which very often thrill the rest of the world in the apprehension of a general war in Europe. We are under no necessity of annexing other territory. We are not afraid of what is called "the balance of power;" we have no army that is worthy of the name, because we don't need one, and we can make one if we should need it; and we have no navy to

speak of, though I think we ought to have for the protection of our commerce, when our commerce shall be further encouraged. We have no entanglements with other nations; the great father of his country in his Farewell Address warned the people against this danger.

4. *Our country is very large.* You school-boys can tell me as well as I can tell you what degrees of latitude and longitude we reach, and how many millions of square miles we count. Europeans say we brag too much about the great extent of our country; but I do not refer to it now for boasting, but as a matter of thankfulness to God for giving it to us. It means that our territory, reaching from the Arctic to the tropics, gives us every variety of climate and almost every variety of product that the earth produces; and I am sure that the time will come when, under a higher agricultural cultivation than we have yet reached, our soil will produce everything that grows anywhere else in the world. The corn harvest now being gathered in our country will reach *two thousand millions of bushels.* The mind staggers under such ponderous figures and quantities. Our wheat fields are hardly less productive; our potatoes and rice and oats and barley and grass, the products of our cattle and sheep, and, in short, everything that our soil above ground yields; and the enormous yield of our coal mines, our oil wells, our natural gas, our metals, our railroads, spanning the entire con-

tinent and binding the people together with bands of steel—all these, and many others, which time will not permit me even to mention, give some faint idea of what a splendid country it is that the Almighty God has given to the American people. And do we not well therefore, when we come together on a day like this, to make our acknowledgments to Him?

5. *The general education of the people* is another reason for thankfulness to God. The system is not yet universal, but it will be at no distant day. You boys will live to see the day when every man, woman and child born in the United States (except those who are too young or feeble-minded) will be able to read and write and cipher. It is sure to come. Then, under the blessing of God, when people learn to do their own reading and thinking, we shall not fear anarchists and atheists and the many other fools who, under one name or another, are now trying to make this people discontented with their lot. There is no need for such people here, and no place for them; they have made a mistake in coming to this free land, as some of them found to their cost on the gallows at Chicago.

6. *We have no war in our country, no famine, and with the exception of poor Jacksonville, Florida, no pestilence.* Famine we have never known, and with such an extent of country we have little need to dread such a scourge as that. No one need suffer for food in our country, and this is the only country

in the world of which this can be said; for labor of some kind can always be found, and food is so cheap, plain kinds of food, that none but the utterly dissipated and worthless need starve; and in fact none do starve; for if they are so wretchedly improvident, the guardians of the poor will save them from suffering not only, but actually provide them with a home, that for real comfort is not known elsewhere in the world.

Some of us have seen war in its most dreadful proportions, but even then the alleviations furnished by the Christian Commission greatly relieved some of its most horrid features; and we are not likely to see war again, for there will be hereafter nothing to quarrel and fight about. Our political differences will never again lead to the taking up of arms in deadly strife.

Such are some of the occasions of thankfulness which led the President of the United States to ask the people, by public proclamation, to turn aside for one day from their business, their farms, their workshops, their counting-houses, to close the schools, and assemble in their places of worship and thank God, the giver of every good and perfect gift.

But I don't think the President of the United States knew what special reasons the Girard College boys have to keep a thanksgiving day. And I shall try in what I have yet to say to point out some of them.

1. This foundation is under the control of the

Board of City Trusts. When Mr. Girard left the bulk of his great estate for this noble purpose, he gave it to the "mayor, aldermen and citizens of Philadelphia," as his trustees. The city of Philadelphia could act only through its legislative body, the select and common councils, bodies elected by the people, and consequently more or less under the influence of one or the other of the great political parties. Nearly twenty years ago, owing largely to Mr. William Welsh, who became the first President of the Board of City Trusts, the legislature of Pennsylvania took from the control of councils all the charitable trusts of the city and committed them to this board. If any political influences were ever unworthily exerted in the former board it ceased when the judges of the city of Philadelphia and the judges of the Supreme Court named the first directors of the City Trusts. These directors are all your friends; they give much thought, much labor, much anxiety to your well-being, desiring to do the best things that are possible to be done for your welfare, and to do them in the best way. Many of them have been successful in finding desirable situations for such of your number as were prepared to accept such places. I am glad to say that I have three college boys associated with me in my business; Mr. Stuart had two; Mr. Michener has two; General Wagner has two, and Mr. Rawle has had one, and probably other members of the board have also, so you see our interest in you is not limited to the time which we spend here and in the office on South Twelfth street, but we are ever on the lookout for things which we hope may be to your advantage.

2. This splendid estate, which you enjoy; these beautiful buildings, which were erected for your use; these grounds, which are so well kept and which are so attractive to you and to the thousands of visitors that come here; these school-rooms, which we determine shall lack nothing that is desirable to make them what they ought to be; the text-books which you use in school, the best that can be found; the teachers, the most accomplished and skilful that can be procured; the prefects and governesses chosen from among many applicants, and because they are supposed to be the best, all your care-takers; all who have to do with you here are chosen because they are supposed to be well qualified to discharge their duties most successfully. The arrangements for your lodging in the dormitories, the furniture and food of your tables, the well-equipped infirmary for the sick, are such as, in the judgment of the trustees, the great founder himself would approve if he could be consulted. Truly, this gives occasion for special thanksgiving on this Thanksgiving Day.

3. *You all have a birthright.*

What that meant in the earliest times we do not fully know; but it meant at least to be the head or father of the family, a sort of domestic priesthood, the chief of the tribe, or the head of a great nation. In our own times, in Great Britain the first-born son has by right of birth the headship of the family, inheriting the principal part of the property, and he is the representative of the estate. They call it there the *law of primogeniture*, or the law of the first-born. In our country there is no birthright in families, and we have no law to make the eldest born in any respect more favored than the other and younger children.

But you Girard boys have a birthright which means a great deal. The founder of this great school left the bulk of his large estate to the city of Philadelphia, for the purpose of adopting and educating a certain class of boys, very particularly described, to which you belong. The provision he made for you was most liberal. Everything that his trustees consider necessary for your careful support and thorough education is to be provided. Nothing is to be wanting which money wisely expended can supply. *This is your birthright.* No earthly power can take it from you without your consent. No commercial distress, no financial panic, no change of political rulers, no combination of party politics can interfere with the purpose of the founder. Nothing but the loss of health or life, or your own misconduct, can deprive you of this great birthright. Do you boys fully appreciate this?

Now, is it to be supposed that there is a boy here who is willing to *sell* this birthright as Esau did?

Is there a boy here who is corrupt in heart, so profane and foul in speech, so vicious in character, so wicked in behavior, as to be an unfit companion for his schoolmates, and who cannot be permitted to remain among them? Is there a boy here who, for the gratification of a vicious appetite, will *sell* that privilege of support and education so abundantly provided here? So guarded is this trust, so sacred almost, that no human being can take it away from you: will you deliberately *throw it away?* The wretched Esau, in the old Jewish history, under the pressure of hunger and faintness, sold his birthright with all its invaluable privileges; will you, with no such temptation as tried him, with no temptation but the perverseness of your own will and your love of self-indulgence, will you *sell your birthright?* Bitterly did Esau regret his folly; earnestly did he try to recover what he had lost, but it was too late; he never did recover his lost birthright, though he sought it carefully and with tears. And he had no one to warn him beforehand as I am warning you.

Boys, if you pass through this college course not making the best use of your time, or if you allow yourselves to fall into such evil habits as will make it necessary to send you away from the college—and this after all the kind words that have been spoken to you and the faithful warnings that have been given you—you will lose that which can never be restored to you, which can never be made up to you in any other way elsewhere. You will prove yourselves more foolish, more wicked than Esau, for you will lose more than he did, and you will do it against kinder remonstrances than he had.

4. There is another feature of the management here which gives especial satisfaction. When a boy leaves the college to go to a place which has been chosen for him, or which he has found by his own exertions, he is looked after until he reaches the age of twenty-one, by an officer especially appointed, and as we believe well adapted to that service. And many a boy who has found himself in unfavorable circumstances and under hard task-masters, with people who have no sympathy with his youth and inexperience, many such have been visited and encouraged, helped and so assisted towards true success.

5. But what is there to make each particular boy thankful to-day? Why you are all in good health; and if you would know how much that means go to the infirmary and see the sick boys there, who are not able to be in the chapel to-day, not able to be in the play-grounds, who are looking out of the windows with wistful eyes, very much desiring to be with you and enjoying your plays but cannot. God bless them.

You are all comfortably clothed; those of you who

PROFESSOR W. H. ALLEN.

are less robust have warmer clothing, and all of you are shielded and guarded as well as the trustees know how to care for you, so that you may be trained to be strong men.

You are all having a holiday; no school to-day; no shop-work to-day; no paying marks to-day; no punishments of any kind to-day. Why? It is Thanksgiving Day and everything that is disagreeable is put out of sight and ought to be put out of mind.

You are all to have a good dinner. Even now, while we are here in the chapel and while some of you are growing impatient at my speech, think of the good dinner that is now cooking for you. Think of the roast turkey, the cranberry sauce, the piping-hot potatoes, the gravy, the dressing, the mince pies, the apples afterwards, and all the other good things which make your mouths water, and make my mouth water even to mention the names. Then after dinner you go to your homes, and you have a good time there.

The last thing I mention which you ought to be thankful for is having a short speech.

# ON THE DEATH OF PRESIDENT ALLEN.

September 24, 1882.

"*Remember how He spake unto you.*"

THESE are the words of an angel. They were spoken in the early morning while it was yet dark, to frightened and sorrowful women, who had gone to the sepulchre of Christ with spices and ointments to embalm his body. These women fully expected to find the body of their Lord; for as they went they said, "Who shall roll us away the stone from the sepulchre?" When they reached the place, they found the stone was rolled away and the grave was empty. And one of them ran back to the disciples to tell them that the grave was open and the body gone. Those that remained went into the sepulchre and saw two men in glittering garments, who, seeing that the women were perplexed and afraid, standing with bowed heads and startled looks, said, with a shade of reproof in their tone, "Why seek ye the living among the dead? He is not here, he is risen." And, perhaps, seeing that the women could hardly believe this, it was added, "Remember how he spake unto you when he was yet in Galilee, saying, 'The Son of man must be delivered into the hands of sinful men, and be crucified, and the third day rise again."

The words that are quoted as having been spoken by Jesus to his disciples were spoken in Galilee six months or more before this, and as they were not clearly understood at the time, it is not so very strange that they should have been forgotten.

It had been well if these sorrowing women, as well as the other disciples of the Lord, had remembered other words, and all the words that the Lord spake to them, not only while in Galilee, but in all other places. The world would be better to-day if those gracious words had been more carefully laid to heart.

I hope the words of my text will bear, without too much accommodation, the use which I shall make of them.

Almost three-quarters of a century ago, a boy was born in the family of a New England farmer. It was in the then territory of Maine, and near the little city of Augusta. The family were plain, poor people, and the child grew up, as many other farmers' children grew up, accustomed to plain living and such work as children could properly be set to do. In the winter he went to school, as well as at other times when the farm work was not pressing. It would be very interesting to know, if we *could* know, whether there was anything peculiar in the early disposition and habits of this boy, or whether he grew up with nothing to distinguish him from his playmates. If we could only know what children would grow up to be distinguished men, we should, I think, be very careful to observe and record any little traits and peculiarities of their early childhood. The boy of whom I am speaking, and whom you know to be William Henry Allen, seems to have been prepared at the academy for college, which he entered at the advanced age of twenty-one years. Four years after, he was graduated, and at once he set out to teach the classics in a little town in the interior of the State of New York. While engaged in that seminary, he was called to a professorship in Dickinson College, at Carlisle, in our own State of Pennsylvania. In Dickinson College he held successively the chairs of chemistry and the natural sciences, and that of English literature, until his resignation, in 1850, to accept the presidency of Girard College.

From this time until his death, except during an interval of five years, his life was spent here. For twenty-seven years he gave himself to the work of organizing and directing the internal affairs of this college, with an interest and efficiency which, until within the last year, never flagged. It is not possible at this day for any of us to appreciate the difficulties he had to encounter in the early days of the college, but we do know that he did the work well.

See how he was prepared for the work he did.

He was a lover of study. When only eight years old he had learned the English grammar so well that his teacher said he could not teach him anything further in that study. There was an old family Bible that was very highly prized by all the family, and his father told him that if he would read that Bible through by the time he was ten years old, it should be his property. The boy did so, and claimed and received his reward. That book is now in the possession of his daughter (Mrs. Sheldon). This early reading of the Bible will, perhaps, account for President Allen's unusual familiarity with the Scriptures, as evinced in the richness of his prayers in this school chapel.

The school to which he went in his early youth was three miles from his father's house; and in all kinds of weather, through the heats of summer and the deep snows of winter, he plodded his way.

I have said that his parents were not rich; and this young man pushed his way through college by teaching, thus earning the money necessary for his support. This may account for the fact that he entered college at the age when most young men are leaving it, viz., twenty-one years. It did not seem to him that it was a great misfortune to be poor; but it was an additional inducement to call forth all his powers to insure success. He knew that he must depend upon himself if he would succeed in life. And so he was not satisfied with qualifying himself for one chair in a college, but, as at Dickinson, he held two or three chairs. He could teach the classics or mathematics or general literature, or chemistry or natural sciences. Not many men had qualities so diversified, or knew so well how to put them to good account. You know very well that this liberal culture was not acquired without hard work. And this hard work he must have done in early life, before cares and duties crowded him, as they will absorb all of us the older we grow.

"Remember how He spake unto you." I would give these words a two-fold meaning—remember *what* he said and *how* he said it.

Twenty-seven years is a long time in the life of any man, even if he has lived more than three-score years and ten. In all these years President Allen was going in and out before the college boys, saying good and kind words to them.

How often he spoke to you in the chapel! It was *your church*, and the only church that you could attend, except on holidays. His purpose was that this chapel service should be worthy of you, and worthy of the day. So important did he consider it, that when his turn came to speak to you here, he prepared himself carefully. He always wrote his little discourses, and the best thoughts of his mind and heart he put into them. He thought that nothing that he or any other speaker could bring was too good for you.

And then the tones of his voice, the manner of his instruction; how gentle, kind, conciliating. He remembered the injunction of Scripture, "The servant of the Lord must not strive." You will never know in this life how much he bore from you, how long he bore with your waywardness, your thoughtlessness; how much he loved you. He always called you "his boys." No matter though some of you are almost men, he always called you "his boys," much as the apostle John in his later years called his disciples his "little children." For President Allen felt that in a certain sense he was a father to you all.

For some time past you knew that his health was declining. You saw his bowed form and his feeble, hesitating steps. In the chapel his voice was tremulous and feeble. The boys on the back benches could not always understand his words distinctly. But you knew that he was in earnest in all that he did say. And for many months he was not able to speak at all in the chapel. On the last Founder's Day he was seated in a chair, with some of his family about him, looking at the battalion boys as they were drilled, but the fatigue was too great for him. And as the summer advanced into August, and the people in his native State were gathering their harvests, he, too, was gathered, as a shock of corn fully ripe.

When Tom Brown heard of the death of his old

master, Arnold of Rugby, he was fishing in Scotland. It was read to him from a newspaper. He at once dropped everything and started for the old school. He was overwhelmed with distress. " When he reached the station he went at once to the school. At the gates he made a dead pause; there was not a soul in the quadrangle, all was lonely and silent and sad; so with another effort he strode through the quadrangle, and into the school-house offices. He found the little matron in her room, in deep mourning; shook her hand, tried to talk, and moved nervously about. She was evidently thinking of the same subject as he, but he couldn't begin talking. Then he went to find the old verger, who was sitting in his little den, as of old.

" ' Where is he buried, Thomas?

" ' Under the altar in the chapel, sir,' answered Thomas. ' You'd like to have the key, I dare say.'

" ' Thank you, Thomas; yes, I should, very much.'

" ' Then,' said Thomas, ' perhaps you'd like to go by yourself, sir?' "

"So he walked to the chapel door and unlocked it, fancying himself the only mourner in all the broad land, and feeding on his own selfish sorrow.

" He passed through the vestibule and then paused a moment to glance over the empty benches. His heart was still proud and high, and he walked up to the seat which he had last occupied as a sixth-form boy, and sat down there to collect his thoughts. The memories of eight years were all dancing through his brain, while his heart was throbbing with a dull sense of a great loss that could never be made up to him. The rays of the evening sun came solemnly through the painted windows over his head and fell in gorgeous colors on the opposite wall, and the perfect stillness soothed his spirit. And he turned to the pulpit and looked at it; and then leaning forward, with his head on his hands, groaned aloud. 'If he could have only seen the doctor for one five minutes, have told him all that was in his heart, what he owed him, how he loved and reverenced him, and would, by God's help, follow his steps in life and death, he could have borne it all without a murmur. But that he should have gone away forever, without knowing it all, was too much to bear.' 'But am I sure that he does not know it all?' The thought made him start. 'May he not even now be near me in this chapel?'"

And with some such feelings as these I suppose many a boy will come back to the college and stand in this chapel, and recall the impressions he has received from President Allen here. But his voice will never be heard here again. Nothing remains but to "remember how he spake unto you."

I am sure you will never forget the day he lay in his coffin in the chapel, and you all looked on his face for the last time. What could be more impressive than the funeral? The crowded house, the waiting people, the bowed heads, the solemn strains of the organ, the sweet voices of children singing their beautiful hymns, the open coffin, the appropriate address given by one of his own college boys, the thousand and more boys standing in open ranks for the procession to pass through to the college gates, the burial at Laurel Hill cemetery, where many of his pupils already lie, and where many more will follow him in the coming years—all these thoughts make that funeral day one long to be remembered.

Let us accept this as the will of Providence. There is nothing to regret for him; but for us, the void left by his withdrawal. He is leading a better life now than ever before. He has just begun to live, and the best words I can say to you are, "remember how he spake unto you."

. . . . . . .

> "But when the warrior dieth,
>     His comrades in the war
> With arms reversed and muffled drums
>     Follow the funeral car.
> They show the banners taken,
>     They tell his battles won,
> And after him lead his masterless steed,
>     While peals the minute gun.
>
> "Amid the noblest of the land
>     Men lay the *sage* to rest,
> And give the *bard* an honored place,
>     With costly marble drest,
> In the great Minster transept
>     Where lights like glories fall,
> And the choir sings and the organ rings
>     Along the emblazoned wall."

# A YOUNG MAN'S MESSAGE TO BOYS.

December 7, 1884.

WHEN I came here in April last I brought with me some friends, among whom was my son. And I said to him that some day I should wish *him* to speak to you. He had so recently been a college boy himself, graduating at the University of Pennsylvania, and he was so fond of the games and plays of boys, and withal was so deeply interested in boys and young men, that I thought he might be able to say something that would interest you, and perhaps do you good.

At a recent meeting of the proper committee his name was added to the list of persons who may be invited to speak to you. The last time I was at the college President Fetterolf asked me when my son could come to address you, and I replied that he was sick.

That sickness was far more serious than any of us supposed; there was no favorable change, and at the end of twelve days he passed away.

My suggestion that he might be invited to speak

here led him to prepare a short address, which was found among his papers, and has, within a few days, been handed to me. It was written with lead pencil, apparently hastily; and certainly lacking the final revision, which in copying for delivery he would have given it.

I have thought it would be well for me to read to you this address; but I did not feel that I had any right to revise it, or to make any change in it whatever; so I give it precisely as he wrote it, adding only a word here and there which was omitted in the hurried writing.

He that is slow to anger is better than the mighty; and he that ruleth his spirit, than he that taketh a city.—Proverbs xvi. 32.

I want you to look with me at the latter part of each of these sentences, and see if we can't understand a little better what Solomon meant by such words "*the mighty*" and "*he that taketh a city.*"

Do you remember the wonderful dream that came to Solomon just after he had been made king over Israel? How God came to him while he was sleeping and said to him, "Ask what I shall give thee," and how Solomon, without any hesitation, asked for wisdom. And God gave him wisdom, so that he became famous far and wide, and people from nations far off came to see him and learn of him.

If I were to ask you now who was the wisest man that ever lived, you would say "Solomon." Often you have heard one person say of another, "he is as wise as Solomon." I cannot stop here to tell you of the way in which Solomon showed this wonderful gift. But his knowledge was not that of books, because there were not a great many books then for him to read. It was the knowledge which showed him how to do *right*, and how to be a *good ruler* over his people. And because he chose such wisdom, the very best gift of God, God gave him besides, riches and everything that he could possibly desire. His horses and chariots were the most beautiful and the strongest; his armies were famous everywhere for their splendid arms and armor. He had vast numbers of servants to wait upon him, and to do his slightest wish. Presents, most magnificent, were sent to him by the kings of all the nations round about him. No king of Israel before or after him was so great and so powerful. And, greatest honor of all, God permitted him to build a temple for him— what his father David had so longed to do and was not allowed, God directed Solomon to do. David's greatest desire before he died was to build a house for God. The ark of God had never had a house to rest in, and David was not satisfied to have a splendid palace to live in himself, and to have nothing but a *tent* in which to keep God's ark. But God would not suffer him to do that, although he was the king whom he loved so much. No, that must be kept for his son Solomon to do. David had been too great a fighter all his life; he had been at war; he had driven back his enemies on all sides, and had made God's people a nation to be feared by all their foes. So David was a "mighty man," and while Solomon was growing up he must have heard every one talking of the wonderful things his father had done from his youth up—the adventures he had had when he was only a poor shepherd lad keeping his flocks on the hills about Bethlehem. And how often must he have been told that splendid story, which we never grow tired of hearing, of his fight with the giant Goliath; and when he was shown the huge pieces of armor, and the great sword and spear, he surely knew what it was for a man to be "mighty" and "great." And when his old father withdrew from the throne and made him king, he found himself surrounded on all sides with the results of his father's wars and conquests, and soon knew that he also was "a mighty man."

There is not a boy here who does not want to be "great." Every one of you wants to make a name for himself, or have something, or do something, that will be remembered long after he is dead.

If I should ask you what that something is, I suppose almost all of you would say, "I want to be rich, so rich that I can do whatever I like; that I need not do any work; that I can go where I please."

Some of you would say, "I would travel all over the world and write about what I see, so that long after I am dead people will read my books and say, 'what a great man he was!'" Some of you would say, "I would build great houses, and fill them with all the richest and most beautiful goods. I would have whole fleets of ships, sailing to all parts of the world, bringing back wonderful things from strange countries; and when I would meet people in the street they would stand aside to let me pass, saying to one another, 'there goes a great man; he is our richest merchant; how I should like to be as great as he.'"

And still another would say: "I don't care anything about books or beautiful merchandise. No, I'll go into foreign countries and become a great fighter, and I shall conquer whole nations, so that my enemies shall be afraid of me, and I shall ride at the head of great armies, and when I come home again the people will give me a grand reception; will make arches across the street, and cover their houses with flags, and as I ride along the street the air will be filled with cheers for the great general."

And so each one of you would tell me of some way in which he would like to be great. I should think very little of the boy who had no ambition, one who would be entirely content to just get along somehow, and never care for any great success so long as he had enough to eat and drink and to clothe himself with, and who would never look ahead to set his mind on obtaining some great object. It is perfectly right and proper to be ambitious, to try and make as much as possible of every opportunity that is presented. No one can read that parable of the master who called his servants to account for the talents he had given them, and not see that God gives us all the blessings and advantages that we have, in order that we may have an opportunity to put them to such good use, that He may say to us as the master in the parable said to his servants, " Well done, good and faithful servant."

So it is right for you to want to be great, and I want to try and tell you how to accomplish it. If you were sure that I could tell you the real secret of success you would listen very carefully to what I had to say, wouldn't you? Some of you would even write down what I said. Then write *this* down in your hearts; for, following this, you will be greater than "the mighty:" " He that is slow to anger is better than the mighty; and he that ruleth his spirit, than he that taketh a city." Are some of you disappointed? do you say, "*Is that all?* I thought he was about to tell us how we could make lots of money." Ah, if you would only believe it, and follow such advice, such a plan were to be far richer than the man who can count his wealth by millions. But look at it in another way. What sort of a boy do you choose for the captain of a base-ball nine or a foot-ball team? What sort of a *man* is chosen for a high position? Is he one who loses all control over himself when something happens to vex him, and flies into a terrible passion when some one happens to oppose him? No; the one you would select for any place of great responsibility is he who can keep his head clear, who will not permit himself to get angry at any little vexation, who rules his own spirit—and can there be anything harder to do? I tell you "no.'

So, I have told you how to be successful, and at the same time I tell you, there is nothing harder to do; and now I go on still further, and say you can't follow such advice by yourself, you must have some help. Is it hard to get? No, it is offered to you freely; you are urged to ask for it, and you are assured that it is certain to come to all who want it. Will such help be sufficient? Much more than sufficient, for He who shall help you is abundantly able to give you more than you ask or think. It is God who tells you to come to him, and he shall make you more than "the mighty," greater than he which taketh the city; yes, for the greatness he shall bestow upon those who come to him is far above all earthly greatness. He shall be with you when you are ready to fly into a furious temper, when you lift your hand to strike, when you would *kill* if you were not afraid; but when the wish is in your heart, yes, then, even then, He is beside you. He looks upon you in divine mercy, and if you will only let him, will rebuke the foul spirit and command him to come out of you, and your whole soul shall be filled with peace. Why won't you listen to his pleading voice, and let him quiet the dreadful storm of anger? And when the hot words fly to your lips, remember his soft answer that turns away wrath. Then will you have won a greater battle than any ever fought; for you will have conquered your own wicked spirit, and by God's grace you are a conqueror. And the reward for a life of such self-conquest shall be a crown of life that fadeth not away. Won't you accept *such* greatness?

Such are the words he would have spoken to you had his life been spared; and he would have spoken them with the great advantage of a *young man* speaking to *young men*. Now they seem like a message from the heavenly world. It is more than probable that in copying for delivery he would have expanded some of the thoughts and have made the little address more complete. Perhaps it would be better for me to stop here; . . but there are a few words which I would like to say, and it may be that they can be better said now than at any other time.

I want to say again, what I have so often said, that a boy may be fond of all innocent games and plays and yet be a Christian. Some of you may doubt this. You may believe and say, that religion interferes with amusements and makes life gloomy.

Here is an example of the contrary; for I do not see how there *could* be a happier life than my son's (there never was a shadow upon it), and no one could be more fond of base-ball and foot-ball and cricket and tennis than he was; and yet he was a simple-hearted Christian boy and young man. And with all this love of innocent pleasure and fun he neglected no business obligations, nor did he fail in any of the duties of social or family life. In short, I can wish no better thing for you boys than that your lives may be as happy and as beautiful as his was.

# A TRUTHFUL CHARACTER.

April, 1889.

CAN anything be more important to a young life than truthfulness? Is character worth anything at all if it is not founded on truth? And are not the temptations to untruthfulness in heart and life constantly in your path?

It is most interesting to think that every life here is an individual life, having its own history, and in many respects unlike every other life. When I see you passing through these grounds, going in procession to and from your school-rooms, your dining halls and your play-grounds, the question often arises in my thoughts, how many of these boys are walking in the truth?

If I were looking for a boy to fill any position within my gift, or within the reach of my influence, and should seek such a boy among you, I should ask most carefully of those who know you best, whether such and such a boy were truthful; and not in speech merely (that is, does he answer questions truthfully), but is he open and frank in his life? Does he cheat in his lessons or in his games? Does he shirk any duty that is required of him in the shops? When he fails to recite his lessons accurately, is he very ready with his excuses trying to justify himself for his failure, or does he admit candidly that he did not do his best, and does he promise sincerely to do better in the future? And is he one who may be depended upon to give a fair account of any incident that may come up for investigation? Sometimes there are wrong things done here, done from thoughtlessness often; may such a boy as I am looking for be depended upon to say what he knows about it, in a manly way, so as to screen the innocent, and, if necessary, expose the guilty? In other words, is he trustworthy, worthy of trust, can he be depended on?

It may not be easy for one at my time of life to say just what a boy ought to be, if he is to make much of a man. But we who think much of this subject have an idea of what we would like the boys to be, in whom we are especially interested. And if I borrow from another a description of what I mean, it is because this author has said it better than I can.

"A real boy should be generous, courteous among his friends and among his school-fellows; respectful to his superiors, well-mannered. He must avoid loud talk and rough ways; must govern his tongue and his temper; must listen to advice and reproof with humility. He must be a gentleman. He must not be a sneak or a bully; he must neither cringe to the strong nor tyrannize over the weak. To his teachers he must be obedient, for they have a right to require obedience of him; he must be respectful, because the true gentleman always respects those who are wiser, more experienced, better informed than himself. He must apply himself to his lessons with a single aim, seeking knowledge for its own sake, and earnestly striving to make the best possible use of such faculties as God has given him. He must do his best to store his mind with high thoughts by a careful study of all that is beautiful and pure. In his sports and plays he must seek to excel, if excellence can be obtained by a moderate amount of time and energy; but he must remember, that though it is a fine thing to have a healthy body and a healthy mind, it is neither necessary nor admirable to develop a muscular system like that of an athlete or a giant. Whatever falls to his hands to do, he must do it with his might, assured that God loves not the idle or dishonest worker. He must remember that life has its duties and responsibilities as well as its pleasures; that these begin in boyhood, and that they cannot be evaded without injury to heart and mind and soul. He must train himself in all good habits, in order that these may accompany him easily in later life; in habits of method and order, of industry and perseverance and patience. He must not forget that every victory over himself smooths the way for future victories of the same kind; and the precious fruit of each moral virtue is to set us on higher and better ground for conquests of principle in all time to come. He must resolutely shut his ears and his heart to every foul word and every improper suggestion, every profane utterance; guarding himself against the first approaches of sin, which are always the most insidiously made. He must not think it a brave or plucky thing to break wholesome rules, to defy authority, to ridicule age or poverty or feebleness, to pamper the appetite, to imitate the 'fast,' to throw away valuable time; to neglect precious opportunities. He must love truth with a deep and passionate love, abhorring even the shadow of a lie, even the possibility of a falsehood. True in word, true in deed, he shall walk in the truth."

I say then to you boys, do your best; be honest and diligent; be resolute to live a pure and honorable life; speak the truth like boys who hope to be gentlemen; be merry if you will, for it is good to be merry and wise; be loving and dutiful sons, be affectionate brothers, be loyal-hearted friends, and when you come to be men you will look back to these boyish days without regret and without shame.

Something like this is my ideal of a boy. I am very desirous that your future shall be bright and useful and successful, and I, and others who are interested in your welfare, will hope to hear nothing but good of you; but we can have no greater joy than to hear that you are walking in the truth. Some of you may become rich men; some may become very prominent in public affairs; you may reach high places; you may fill a large space in the public estimation; you may be able and brilliant men; but there is nothing in your life that will give us so much joy as to hear that "you are walking in the truth."

Truth is the foundation of all the virtues, and without it character is absolutely worthless. No gentleness of disposition, no willingness to help other people, no habits of industry, no freedom from vicious practices, can make up for want of truthfulness of heart and life. Some persons think that if they work long and hard and deny themselves for the good of others, and do many generous and noble acts and have a good reputation, they can even tell lies sometimes and not be much blamed. But they forget that reputation is not character; that one may have a very good reputation and a very bad character; they forget that the reputation is the outside, what we see of each other, while the character is what we are in the heart.